THE CHAMPIONSHIPS
WIMBLEDON
Official Annual 2003

JOHN PARSONS

Photographs by

CLIVE BRUNSKILL, PHIL COLE, MIKE HEWITT, ALEX LIVESEY
of GETTY IMAGES

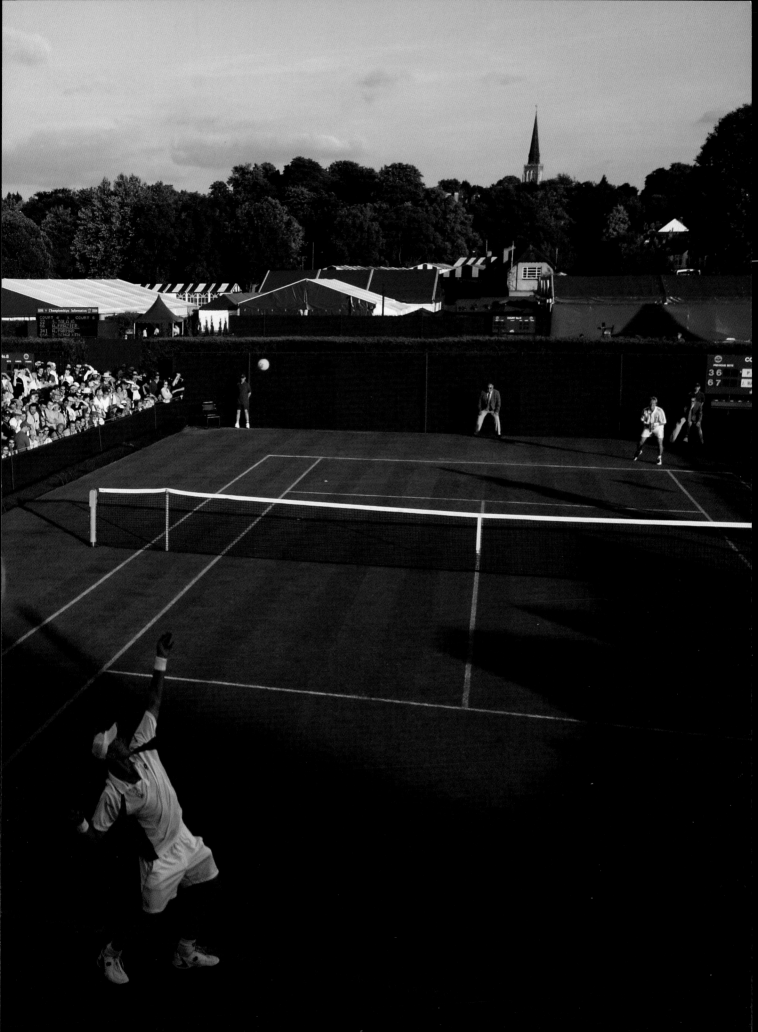

Publisher
ROBERT YARHAM

Publishing Development Manager
PETER MERCER

Art Editor
STEVE SMALL

Publicity and promotion
ANNALISA ZANELLA

Photography
CLIVE BRUNSKILL
PHIL COLE
MIKE HEWITT
ALEX LIVESEY

Photo Research, Getty Images
ELAINE LOBO
KER ROBERTSON

This first edition published in 2003 by Hazleton Publishing Ltd,
5th Floor, Mermaid House, 2 Puddle Dock, London EC4V 3DS

Hazleton Publishing Ltd is part of
Profile Media Group Plc

ISBN: 1-903135-29-X

Printed in England by Butler and Tanner Ltd,
Frome, Somerset

Colour reproduction by Radstock Repro Ltd,
Midsomer Norton, Somerset

Results tables are reproduced by courtesy of
The All England Lawn Tennis Club

This book is produced with the assistance of Rolex

ROLEX

FOREWORD

The 117th Championships began and ended with sensations.

In the first match of the tournament on Centre Court, defending champion Lleyton Hewitt was dethroned in four sets by qualifier Ivo Karlovic, who is almost one foot taller (28 cm) than the Australian.

Then in the last match, the mixed doubles final also on Centre Court, Martina Navratilova (partnered by Leander Paes) won her 20th Wimbledon title — 27 years after she won her first. She thereby equalled Billie Jean King's record of 20 Championship titles at Wimbledon and the capacity crowd loved this nostalgic climax to Wimbledon 2003.

In between these two dramatic matches, the second highest aggregate crowds in Wimbledon history were able to enjoy a feast of tennis of the highest quality.

Our two singles champions are both only 21 years old. Serena Williams is the world number one-ranked player and with her win she has now won five of the last six Grand Slam ladies' singles titles. To take the title she had to beat Jennifer Capriati, Justine Henin-Hardenne and, finally, sister Venus. This she did with great power and athleticism.

In the men's singles, Roger Federer came through to win for the loss of only one set in the tournament. His talent has never been in doubt but he played tennis of such sublime quality and variety that the Wimbledon crowds took him to their hearts. In particular, during his semi-final win against Andy Roddick, he played tennis that could bear comparison with any of the great Centre Court exponents of the past. And so, five years after he became the Junior Wimbledon Champion, Roger Federer became the first Swiss men's singles champion.

Todd Woodbridge and Jonas Bjorkman defended their men's doubles title. Todd has now won eight Wimbledon men's doubles Championships, a feat only ever equalled by the Doherty brothers between 1897 and 1905.

The ladies' doubles title was won by Kim Clijsters and Ai Sugiyama in considerable style. This demonstrated yet again the international competitiveness of tennis — the eight different players who won the five Championship titles this year came from seven different countries.

I am sure you will find this annual fun to read as it tells the story of Wimbledon 2003.

Tim Phillips
Chairman of The All England Lawn Tennis & Croquet Club
and the Committee of Management of The Championships

INTRODUCTION

The build-up to Wimbledon 2003 was more of a tease than most. In the three weeks before The Championships began, the domination by the Williams sisters among the ladies had been brought into question and weighing up the evidence among the men was about as straightforward as trying to pick the right six lottery numbers.

Lleyton Hewitt, the defending champion, not only lost his title at the Stella Artois Championships at Queen's Club, where the results can often be a reasonable guide to Wimbledon prospects but he was overtaken by 33-year-old Andre Agassi on top of the world rankings.

True, Andy Roddick had provided timely and credible evidence in support of his bid by winning at Queen's, especially by beating Agassi in the semi-finals but there was still the belief that any one among a dozen men could take the crown. Agassi, Roddick, and the richly talented but unpredictable Swiss player, Roger Federer, were obvious contenders at the top of the list, followed by Tim Henman, Britain's most consistent challenger for almost 70 years, and unseeded, dangerous floaters such as Mark Philippoussis and Greg Rusedski.

There was even the thought that perhaps, after the way David Nalbandian had steadfastly worked his way through to the final a year earlier that even he, or one or more of the other South Americans who might have been inspired by him, might shine on the grass this time.

And what about Juan Carlos Ferrero, the elegant Spaniard who had just won the French Open and talked about wanting to prove his abilities on all surfaces? There was also the intriguing possibility that Holland's 6ft 5in Martin Verkerk, who had suddenly come to the fore in recent months and been runner-up in Paris, could use his ferocious serves and scorching returns just as successfully on grass, despite his almost total lack of experience on the surface and his self-confessed problem 'that I don't find it easy to bend down as much as I will have to at Wimbledon.'

Picking a likely winner was not made easier by examining the top eight listed among the seeds. Even with the seeding formula that sensibly allows performances on grass during the two previous years to carry more weight, the list included a preponderance of names noted more for their success on clay courts than faster surfaces.

Yet it was not with hindsight that on Day One I tipped Serena Williams and Federer to be the champions, saying of the latter 'He has the perfect game for grass, including the widest repertoire of skilfully created shots, emphasised by his wonderful authority on both flanks.' As we know now, neither disappointed.

Agassi, naturally enough, was the sentimental favourite. Wimbledon is always one of the key targets in the year for the 1992 champion, who was also runner-up in 1999, or at least it has been since he realised how much he was missing by staying away in the late 1980s, after losing ignominiously in the first round of his premier visit in 1987.

'It rained a lot. I told myself my game wasn't designed for a surface which demands a great deal of coming forward and swore I'd never be back,' he said. 'I'm older and more mature now and fully aware of the place Wimbledon has in the game. It has its own magic. To me, being on Centre Court is the greatest feeling in the world.'

Writing off any defending champion before a tournament starts is always a risky business but serious doubts about Hewitt's chances were expressed well before his opening-day calamity. The previous few months had hardly been plain sailing for him. He had gambled on playing only one tournament before the French Open and it backfired. His form there was scrappy and after Queen's Club, where he was comprehensively outpaced and outwitted by Frenchman, Sebastien Grosjean, John Lloyd, the former British Davis Cup player, described his tennis as 'awful' and added 'He'll need to improve his game by 20 per cent in time for Wimbledon.' Yet there was just as much possibility that Hewitt had not wanted to peak too soon and was keeping his powder dry for the tournament that means most to him.

It would have been nice to think that either Henman or Rusedski could at last provide a British men's singles winner for the first time since Fred Perry in 1936, or the first men's finalist since Bunny Austin in 1938. Henman was confident that his game had started to fall back into shape following his shoulder surgery and Rusedski created pre-Wimbledon excitement by winning 48 hours earlier at Nottingham. After what had been through, however, most felt it was expecting too much.

Despite the events in Paris, where Venus Williams lost to a Russian teenager in the fourth round and Serena to Justine Henin-Hardenne amid difficult circumstances in the semi-finals, everything still pointed not only to Serena deservedly being the favourite to keep her Wimbledon crown but to older sister, Venus, again being on the other side of the net for the final.

There was a firm impression that having completed what was dubbed 'the Serena Slam' by adding the Australian Open title in January, to those of the French Open, Wimbledon and US Open she had won in 2002, Serena's focus going into the French Open this year may have slipped. Wimbledon 2003 would demonstrate whether tennis had lost some of its appeal for her, or if losing in Paris, which after all was only her third defeat in 39 matches, would prove to have been a wake-up call.

Asked on the eve of The Championships how long it had taken her to get over her defeat at Roland Garros, Serena thought for a moment and then said knowingly, 'All of 20 minutes. What happened in Paris stays in Paris.'

Not that Serena's obvious confidence diminished the prospects of Henin-Hardenne, a former finalist who had already beaten her twice earlier in the year, or Kim Clijsters, whose attacking game many felt would surely flourish to the full on grass one day. It would also be fascinating to see how many from among a rich batch of young Russians making impressive headway, including the often noisily charismatic 16-year-old, Maria Sharapova, would make the most impact.

Everything, including the weather for the first week, was set for an exciting, enthralling fortnight. Not even the eve-of-tournament threat from members of ATP that some of their players might boycott The Championships in 2004 and stage their own event elsewhere, if their considerable financial demands were not met, overshadowed the tennis.

Sit back now and enjoy this record of how another memorable Wimbledon unfolded.

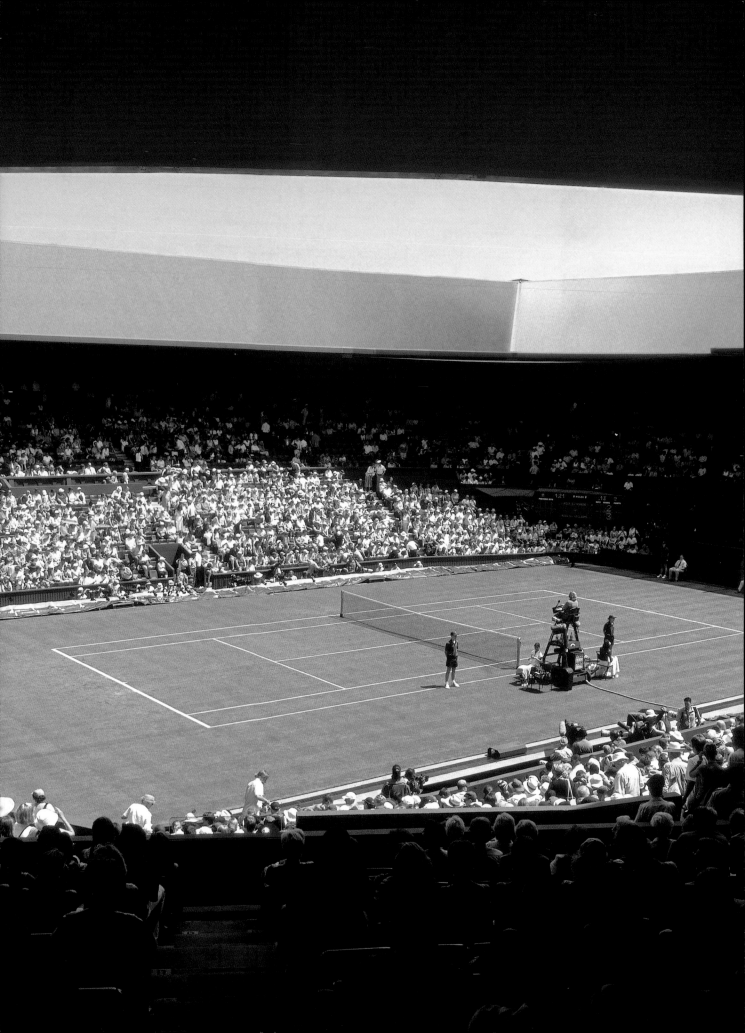

THERE IS A MOMENT WHEN YOU BECOME
PART OF TIME.
AND A MOMENT WHEN YOU BECOME
PART OF HISTORY.

There is only one Wimbledon. And in the hearts of those who play and dream, there is only one Centre Court. It is the place where legends come of age. Where a select few have been able to reach down, seize the moment, and surpass even their own expectations. It is where, for just an instant, the whole world is watching, and we as mere mortals find it quite impossible to look away. **THE WIMBLEDON CHAMPIONSHIPS – JUNE 23RD TO JULY 6TH, 2003.**

OYSTER PERPETUAL DATEJUST · WWW.ROLEX.COM

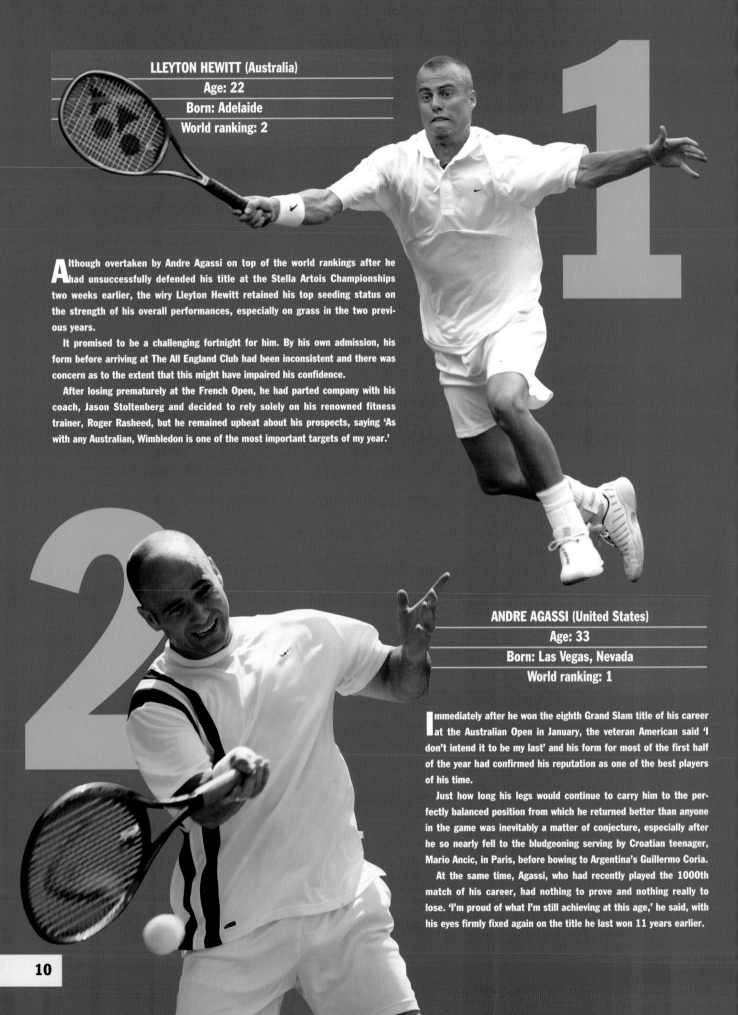

LLEYTON HEWITT (Australia)
Age: 22
Born: Adelaide
World ranking: 2

1

Although overtaken by Andre Agassi on top of the world rankings after he had unsuccessfully defended his title at the Stella Artois Championships two weeks earlier, the wiry Lleyton Hewitt retained his top seeding status on the strength of his overall performances, especially on grass in the two previous years.

It promised to be a challenging fortnight for him. By his own admission, his form before arriving at The All England Club had been inconsistent and there was concern as to the extent that this might have impaired his confidence.

After losing prematurely at the French Open, he had parted company with his coach, Jason Stoltenberg and decided to rely solely on his renowned fitness trainer, Roger Rasheed, but he remained upbeat about his prospects, saying 'As with any Australian, Wimbledon is one of the most important targets of my year.'

2

ANDRE AGASSI (United States)
Age: 33
Born: Las Vegas, Nevada
World ranking: 1

Immediately after he won the eighth Grand Slam title of his career at the Australian Open in January, the veteran American said 'I don't intend it to be my last' and his form for most of the first half of the year had confirmed his reputation as one of the best players of his time.

Just how long his legs would continue to carry him to the perfectly balanced position from which he returned better than anyone in the game was inevitably a matter of conjecture, especially after he so nearly fell to the bludgeoning serving by Croatian teenager, Mario Ancic, in Paris, before bowing to Argentina's Guillermo Coria.

At the same time, Agassi, who had recently played the 1000th match of his career, had nothing to prove and nothing really to lose. 'I'm proud of what I'm still achieving at this age,' he said, with his eyes firmly fixed again on the title he last won 11 years earlier.

JUAN CARLOS FERRERO (Spain)
Age: 22
Born: Onteniente
World ranking: 3

The elegantly stylish Juan Carlos Ferrero had committed himself the previous winter to a fitness and general training programme designed to bring him not only outstanding success on clay but on any surface. The first half of the year indicated that the effort had been worthwhile.

He had played superbly throughout the French Open to win his first Grand Slam title — one that he might easily have claimed 12 months earlier but for injury in the final. He had upgraded all aspects of his game, especially his serve, without losing any of the strength or subtlety from his groundstrokes and his ability to play an increasing variety of shots almost at will.

No Spaniard had won Wimbledon since Manuel Santana in 1966 but with modern tennis balls taking some of the pace out of the game, there were many ready to tip Ferrero to become the first man since Bjorn Borg to win the French Open and Wimbledon in the same year.

ANDY RODDICK (United States)
Age: 20
Born: Omaha, Nebraska
World ranking: 6

After a mixed start to the year, the odds against Andy Roddick winning Wimbledon had been slashed dramatically from 25-1 to 7-2 in less than a week while he was thumping down aces galore on his way to winning the Stella Artois title at Queen's Club.

Since he first made an impact as a raw youngster three years earlier, he had been heralded as potentially the next American men's world champion, once the impetuosity in his naturally aggressive, wonderfully exciting approach to the game could be controlled.

He also arrived for the grass-court season with a new coach, Brad Gilbert, hardly the most patient player himself but, as he had proved while working with Andre Agassi, one capable of blending talents to make a great champion.

Roddick's greatest strength is his serve. Against Agassi at Queen's he hit 29 aces, plus he equalled Greg Rusedski's world delivery record of 149 mph.

ROGER FEDERER (Switzerland)
Age: 21
Born: Basle
World ranking: 5

Since the premature retirement of former Wimbledon champion, Martina Hingis, a few months earlier, at the age of 22, Switzerland's tennis hopes landed principally on Roger Federer's shoulders.

His talent has never been in question. His ability to play on grass was demonstrated when he won the junior boys' singles title in 1998 but he had been taking longer than many had predicted to break through to the very top.

In 2002, his Grand Slam record included first-round defeats at both the French Open and Wimbledon. He had also lost in the first round of the French this year. Yet his outstanding Davis Cup record —13 singles wins from 14 rubbers — shot down those who wondered if he had the temperament for the big occasion.

Federer arrived at Wimbledon 2003 having already won four tournaments on four different surfaces, including grass in Halle two weeks before Wimbledon, with the knowledge that he was running into the best form of his career.

DAVID NALBANDIAN (Argentina)
Age: 21
Born: Cordoba
World ranking: 9

David Nalbandian admitted that life had never been quite the same since his achievement a year earlier in becoming the first South American to reach the Wimbledon final in the Open era. He became an instant sporting hero in his own country and returned to The Championships promising that he intended to be just as significant a threat this time.

Although lacking the customary qualities expected for major success on grass, he does have almost unlimited stamina, fighting spirit and a cool nerve as he illustrated a year earlier in winning back-to-back five-set matches against Nicolas Lapentti and Xavier Malisse.

Far from fading away after making such a major breakthrough at The Championships in 2002, the resolute baseliner, who won the boys' doubles at Wimbledon in 1999, with Guillermo Coria, began this year by beating Roger Federer on his way to the quarter finals of the Australian Open.

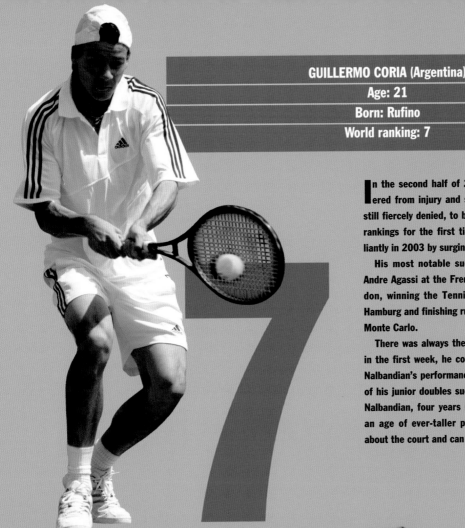

GUILLERMO CORIA (Argentina)
Age: 21
Born: Rufino
World ranking: 7

In the second half of 2002, Guillermo Coria had recovered from injury and suspension for a drug offence he still fiercely denied, to break into the top 50 of the world rankings for the first time and had maintained that brilliantly in 2003 by surging into the top ten.

His most notable successes had included outplaying Andre Agassi at the French Open a month before Wimbledon, winning the Tennis Masters Series tournament in Hamburg and finishing runner-up to Juan Carlos Ferrero at Monte Carlo.

There was always the possibility that if he started well in the first week, he could find himself inspired by David Nalbandian's performances a year earlier and the memory of his junior doubles success at Wimbledon, partnered by Nalbandian, four years previously. Although diminutive in an age of ever-taller players, he is exceptionally quick about the court and can play with considerable finesse.

SJENG SCHALKEN (Netherlands)
Age: 26
Born: Weert
World ranking: 12

This lanky, upright right-hander from Holland, living in Monte Carlo, had figured in several notable matches at Wimbledon, where his ferocious serving makes him one of the most feared by the most highly ranked in the tournament.

In 2000 he had featured in a thrilling third-round match against Mark Philippoussis that lasted 5 hours 5 minutes, the second longest on record at the tournament, before losing the fifth set 20-18. In 2002, he collected a 12-2 match record on grass, with Lleyton Hewitt, the eventual world champion, the only player to beat him on the surface.

Their clash in the quarter-finals at Wimbledon was one of the finest matches of the fortnight. He recovered from two sets down and in the fifth not only twice failed to capitalise on breaks to the Hewitt serve but also missed a point in the 11th game that would have enabled him to serve for the match. He may not be champion material but is well capable of upsetting the biggest names.

SERENA WILLIAMS (United States)
Age: 21
Born: Sanigaw, Michigan
World ranking: 1

Disappointed by having her run of four consecutive Grand Slam victories ended by Justine Henin-Hardenne in the semi-finals of the French Open a month earlier, Serena Williams arrived at Wimbledon clearly determined to demonstrate that she was still the best lady player in the world.

For her, the set-back in Paris had been a minor blip, possibly even a timely reminder that, despite the extent of her domination in the previous year, she could not afford to relax if she wanted the situation to stay that way.

Her principal task when she returned home to Florida between the French Open and Wimbledon was to work on a serve that had suddenly lost its sting and reliability. Even so she was still clearly the player to beat, especially on a surface so suited to her aggressive, powerful game. Far from worrying her, the fact that she was drawn in the same half as Henin-Hardenne for The Championships seemed to add inspiration.

KIM CLIJSTERS (Belgium)
Age: 20
Born: Bilzen
World ranking: 2

Kim Clijsters was the only one among the quartet at the top of the ladies' rankings without a Grand Slam title. She had been close several times, having twice lost in the final of the French Open, a month earlier and also in 2001 when she lost an epic final set to Jennifer Capriati, 12-10.

Yet that and her failure to beat Serena in the semi-finals of the Australian Open after she led 5-1 in the final set, left some to wonder about her temperament for the biggest occasions.

It was a major setback during a period of considerable success. Between November and mid-March, at last clear of stress fracture problems in her arm and shoulder, she reached seven finals in nine tournaments and won five titles, ending the year with a flourish. During the WTA end-of-the-season Championships in Los Angeles, she collected her first major title by beating Serena in the final. Yet a Slam remained an elusive target.

JUSTINE HENIN-HARDENNE (Belgium)

Age: 21

Born: Liège

World ranking: 3

Though standing barely 5ft 5in tall, Justine Henin-Hardenne had never allowed her slender physique to hold her back. During the break between the 2002–2003 seasons, she had spent what was effectively an extended honeymoon in America working intensely on building up her physical strength.

In the months that followed the benefits quickly became apparent. Although losing to Kim Clijsters in the final of Antwerp, she won three of her next five tournaments and then crowned the first half of the year by winning the French, where she beat Serena Williams for the second time in the year.

Henin-Hardenne compensates for her lack of height and reach by being one of the quickest and most agile players round the court. Perfect timing from the back of the court often forces her opponents onto the back foot, while her one-handed backhand is one of the most impressive in the game, but the second serve and volley still need to be improved for Wimbledon to be a likely prize.

VENUS WILLIAMS (United States)

Age: 23

Born: Lynwood, California

World ranking: 4

There had been fears in the months between the Australian Open and Wimbledon that, apart from struggling with a variety of injuries, most notably recurring strained stomach muscles, Venus Williams had lost some of her enthusiasm for the game.

Having lost four times in succession in Grand Slam finals, and the world number one ranking, to her younger sister, Serena, it would not have been surprising. Yet after a disastrous time at the French Open where, according to Serena, she was in such pain from the injury that she should not have played and she was beaten in the fourth round by a teenage Russian, rookie Vera Zvonareva, Wimbledon would clearly be a testing time for her.

The opportunity for quick revenge against Zvonareva provided by the draw had whetted her appetite. Her grass-court pedigree was indisputable. After all she had won Wimbledon in 2000 and 2001. Why could she not do so again?

15

5

LINDSAY DAVENPORT (United States)
Age: 27
Born: Palos Verdes, California
World ranking: 5

Lindsay Davenport remains one of the most powerful hitters in the game although a major knee injury which prevented her from playing in three of the Grand Slam tournaments in 2002, including Wimbledon, had meant her falling out of the top ten for the first time in eight years.

There had also been major changes in both her professional and personal life. She had amicably parted company with her long-serving coach, Robert Van't, who felt he needed to travel less and spend more time with his growing family. She had then worked for a few months with former Wimbledon doubles champion, Rick Leach, brother of Jon, who Lindsay married just ahead of the French Open.

Although still not back to the form that made her Wimbledon champion in 1999 and the runner-up a year later, she had nevertheless done well enough on the tour in the first half of the year, winning one title and being in three other finals, to be a serious title contender.

7 *

CHANDA RUBIN (United States)
Age: 27
Born: Lafayette, Louisiana
World ranking: 8

Two days before The Championships began, Chanda Rubin had boosted her confidence by retaining the Eastbourne title, albeit after a two-hour delay created by a security scare, for the second year in succession.

From the moment she first burst on the scene, Rubin has always been one of the most attractive players on the WTA Tour, moving and striking the ball with a grace one felt belonged only to a bygone age. Just how much more success she might have achieved but for a hand injury, which inhibited her for two years just after she had reached the semi-finals of the Australian Open and led Monica Seles 5-2 in the final set, can only be conjecture.

She may lack the weight of shot of other competitors but never stamina or fitness. In 1995 at Wimbledon she won one of the longest ladies' matches played at The All England Club, lasting over three hours. A few months later she won a final set 16-14 against Arantxa Sanchez-Vicario at the Australian Open.

Amelie Mauresmo, seeded six, withdrew injured.

JENNIFER CAPRIATI (United States)
Age: 27
Born: New York
World ranking: 7

Although twice winner at the Australian Open and once at the French, the prodigy who lost her way but courageously pulled herself back on track was again to be disappointed that Wimbledon and the US Open, the two that would have counted most for her, continued to elude her.

Jennifer Capriati is best remembered at Wimbledon for becoming, at 15, the youngest semi-finalist in the ladies' singles, after giving the defending champion, Martina Navratilova, her earliest defeat at The Championships for 15 years. Despite recurring inconsistency problems with her serve, she had advanced to the semi-finals again in 2001 and was certainly more than just an outside bet for the title.

Her sturdy frame has proved to be a help in terms of giving her tremendous power in her shots from the back of the court though it can sometimes be a hindrance in as much that she has to train harder than most to keep her weight in check.

Since making her breakthrough at the Australian Open in January 2002 and underlining her rapid progress by winning the first title of her career at Indian Wells two months later, Daniela Hantuchova had become a player appreciated by spectators and court-side photographers alike.

Yet for much of 2003, the admiration turned into growing concern when she was unable to regain any of the weight she had lost from her already wafer-thin frame during major training sessions in the South African heat over Christmas.

Although still able to deliver ferocious forehands, her results during the first half of 2003 had been disappointing by her standards.

She was gaining a reputation for losing too many important matches after being in a winning position, not least against the American, Ashley Harkleroad in the second round of the French Open, making it an increasing worry for her British coach, Nigel Sears.

DANIELA HANTUCHOVA (Slovak Republic)
Age: 20
Born: Poprad
World ranking: 9

THE CHAMPIONSHIPS WIMBLEDON

MONDAY 23 JUNE

Day 1

The champion, Lleyton Hewitt, slain by a giant, Ivo Karlovic.

Ivo Karlovic (above) raises his arms at his
moment of record-breaking triumph.

Day 1 • Hewitt v Karlovic

Lleyton Hewitt's shock first-round defeat did not prevent the defending champion from starring in another sporting role during the fortnight. Playing in the annual cricket match between Australian and South African players on the middle Sunday, he took four wickets for 13 as South Africa were bowled out for 155, chasing Australia's 184 for six.

At 3.28 pm on the opening day, an astonished and admiring Centre Court crowd leapt to their feet to acknowledge an achievement that meant Wimbledon 2003 had already made history.

Ivo Karlovic, a 24-year-old Croatian qualifier, placed 203 in the world rankings, had just sent a scorching, unreturnable forehand deep into Lleyton Hewitt's backhand corner — and, for the first time since tennis went Open in 1968, the reigning men's singles champion had fallen at the first hurdle in the defence of his title, losing to Karlovic 1-6, 7-6(7-5), 6-3, 6-4.

Hewitt, at 5ft 11in, is not exactly little but Karlovic, at 6ft 10in, the tallest player ever to compete on the professional circuit, is unmistakably large and he had not only grown in confidence during the match but also in stature as he effectively transformed himself from a giant non-entity to world sporting recognition.

The only other time the defending champion had lost his opening match was in 1967, one year before amateurs and professionals were first allowed to compete against each other. Then Spain's Manuel Santana lost to the serve-and-volleying American, Charlie Pasarell.

To some extent, that upset 36 years earlier was not a massive shock, certainly not in view of what had happened in the previous 2 hours 20 minutes. Hewitt romped through the opening set in 25 minutes, had enough break points early in the second to have fully stamped his authority on the match but then succumbed to an opponent making his Wimbledon and Grand Slam debut after failing on ten earlier attempts to qualify for one of them.

Hewitt, clearly apprehensive before going on court against such a towering opponent who had hit 81 aces during his three qualifying matches at Roehampton, had tried to elicit some tips on how to play Karlovic from another big-serving Croatian, Mario Ancic. He, after all, had bludgeoned enough big serves past Roger Federer to create one of the most significant first-round shocks a year earlier.

All went well early on when Karlovic, who must have felt he had been swept out of his normal environment and deposited in a different

No lack of British and Canadian support for Greg Rusedski (above) as he won three close sets against Alexander Waske on a day when Andy Roddick's serve was too much for Davide Sanguinetti (far right).

24

world, was a bag of nerves. After all, here he was, a rookie in terms of registering success, who had averaged less than £20,000 a year in prize money during his career, facing a world champion who had already earned £6.8m. And they were playing on the most famous tennis court in the world.

Maybe Hewitt, one of five men's seeds beaten on Day One, was given a false sense of security by the ease with which he won the first set. On the other hand his pre-Wimbledon form had not been convincing and, when the break points in the second set eluded him, the doubts re-emerged, encouraging Karlovic, whose serve was by now firing on all cylinders, to make his move.

'That first set I was scared but after that I saw that I can beat him. I start to play better,' he said. That was an understatement. Steadily during the third set and even more so in the fourth, Karlovic was not only dominating with his serve but ruthlessly attacking the Hewitt backhand at every opportunity. By the end the approach shots, the volleys, the overheads and the drop shots were all of the highest quality, demonstrating that even a player with talent but no track record can thrive once confidence kicks in.

Another Croatian, Ivan Ljubicic, also enjoyed the opening day, surviving the formidable serving power of American, Taylor Dent, 7-5, 3-6, 6-3, 7-5 though ironically Ancic, the 2002 first-round shock winner, found himself upstaged this time by a newcomer — Spain's 17-year-old Rafael Nadal. The left-hander, who had first come to prominence at the Monte Carlo Open in April, when he upset both Albert Costa and Carlos Moya, was anything but timid when confronted by the Ancic serve, and took full advantage when his opponent strode to the net to display his already refined passing qualities.

The final game was typical. One top-spin forehand from Nadal had so much whip on it that Ancic swung at the ball but missed completely. The Spaniard, making his Grand Slam debut, then underlined his supremacy with a full-length diving forehand and was lying prostrate on the ground when the ball swept past the Croatian as the non-Croatians among the crowd also cherished the moment.

Roger Federer and Andy Roddick, the two most likely beneficiaries of Hewitt's abrupt dismissal, were happy after clearing their first hurdles but agreed that the defeat of the defending champion had happened too soon in the fortnight for it necessarily to make life easier for them.

Federer, who knew of Hewitt's exit moments before walking onto court for his 6-3, 6-3, 7-6 (7-2) victory over the Korean, Hyung-Taik Lee, said 'I have an outside chance — maybe no bigger but I can't really focus on winning the tournament yet. The road ahead is too long.'

Roddick started well in his 6-2, 6-3, 6-3 win against Italy's Davide Sanguinetti and did nothing to disappoint those who had decided he was worth a bet after his outstanding performances on the way to winning the Stella Artois title at Queen's Club.

Two British men carried the Union flag into the second round, Greg Rusedski, apparently thriving in his new role as a dangerous floater in the draw and the Somerset six-footer, Lee Childs.

Unseeded after two operations that had prevented him playing for nine months, Rusedski overcame the German, Alexander Waske 7-6 (8-6), 7-5, 7-6 (9-7) but at times it was a bumpy ride. Although the British number two started with three aces and another delivery that almost shaved the paint off Waske's racket, the serving power was far from confined to one side of the net. Waske also began with three aces, setting the pattern for the opening set although thankfully there was more variety in the tie-break when volleys were exchanged and Rusedski clinched it with a magnificent backhand pass.

One break gave Rusedski the second set, though only after he had saved a break point. There were more chances for Waske in the third but Rusedski's booming aces proved decisive, even though he acknowledged that his all-round game would have to be stronger when he tackled Roddick two days later.

Childs, who had already taken two important tie-breaks, raised his game impressively on Court 13 to set up his thrilling 2-6, 7-6 (7-2), 1-6, 7-6 (7-5), 6-2 victory over the 33rd seed, Nikolay Davydenko, a Russian

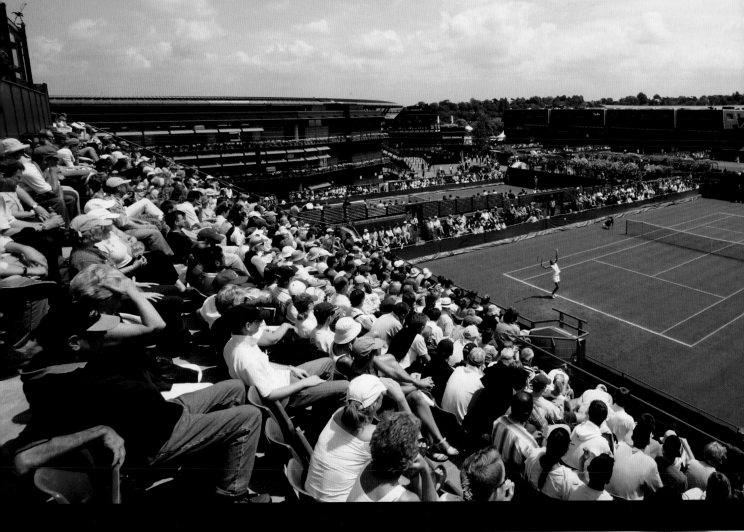

British players were out in force, as were the crowds on Day One supporting (clockwise from top right) Arvind Parmar, Anne Keothavong, Lucie Ahl, Lee Childs who upset Russian seed, Nikolay Davydenko, and Alan Mackin.

v Stosur

The first round is often tough business, as demonstrated (clockwise from the left) by Venus Williams, Stanislava Hrozenska, Lindsay Davenport and Vera Zvonareva.

ranked 452 places above him to register his first win at The Championships — and his first at a main event on grass.

His 13th ace in the opening game of the final set enabled him to escape a crucial break point and he also enjoyed a timely slice of good fortune when he retrieved a Davydenko smash and his shot clipped the top of the net before dropping on what for him was the right side of the net.

Scotland's Alan Mackin had been the first British wild card to depart the tournament losing in less than two hours on Court 14 to the Brazilian, Flavio Saretta, 6-2, 6-4, 6-2, while Arvind Parmar went down 6-3, 6-4, 6-1 to the heavy-serving Dutchman, Sjeng Schalken, and there was no joy either for Lucie Ahl or Anne Keothavong. The latter, recently installed as the new British number one was trailing 6-2, 4-0 to Slovakia's Katarina Srebotnik when she had to retire with a recurrence of her wrist injury. Ahl was disappointingly eclipsed 3-6, 6-4, 6-4 by Ai Sugiyama after holding a final set break against the Japanese 13th seed.

As the shock waves from Hewitt's display continued to reverberate, there was obviously interest in how his girlfriend, Kim Clijsters, would react when she followed him onto Centre Court to play Rossana Neffa-De Los Rios. The answer was that the only competitor from Paraguay in this year's draw felt the full force of a ruthless Clijster's backlash. The world number two insisted that she gained no extra motivation from Hewitt's defeat. Even so it took her only 33 minutes to trounce a bemused opponent, 6-0, 6-0.

Similarly, fourth-seeded Venus Williams, still concerned about how long her strained stomach muscles would enable her to play without pain, coasted through her opening match on Court Two, beating the 184-ranked Slovakian qualifier, Stanislava Hrozenska, 6-2, 6-2 in 53 minutes. By contrast another former champion, Lindsay Davenport, found the Australian wild card Samantha Stosur altogether more stubborn before edging home 7-6 (7-3), 7-5, while seventh-seeded Chanda Rubin, the Eastbourne champion a week earlier, showed plenty of style in her 6-3, 6-0 defeat of the 1997 French Open champion, Iva Majoli.

THE CHAMPIONSHIPS WIMBLEDON

TUESDAY 24 JUNE

Day 2

'The Grand Slam tournaments all have special moments but Wimbledon's electric episodes are remarkably uncluttered, free of commercial intrusion. While the US Open seems like one big marketing opportunity, interrupted by a tennis match once in a while, the sport is first and last at Wimbledon.'

Lisa Dillman of the 'LA Times', writing in 'The Guardian' on the eve of the tournament.

After the stunning exit of Lleyton Hewitt the day before, the upsets on Day Two, though naturally distressing to the victims, were very much of a secondary nature in both the men's and women's singles.

Six men's seeds were beaten, included fierce-serving Dutchman, Martin Verkerk, runner-up at the French Open just over two weeks earlier, but there was nothing to distract domestic attention from Tim Henman's somewhat shaky start to his tenth Wimbledon campaign.

Although he was never in serious danger of losing to Tomas Zib, the 27-year-old Czech lucky loser from qualifying who had won only one match on the main tour earlier in the year and never recorded a victory in a Grand Slam, Henman's win was much more of a struggle than either he or his supporters at Court One and on 'Henman Hill' would have wished.

When he sailed through the first set and led 4-2 in the second, with a point on his own serve for 5-2, it looked as if Henman would progress in style. Instead, in his own words, it became 'a bit of a dogfight' during the rest of the second set and the third before he completed a 6-2, 7-6 (13-11), 3-6, 6-1 success in a flourish.

Henman's inconsistency was first demonstrated in the middle of the second set. Having played exquisite backhands, two of them dipping and dying on the still-lush grass, as he broke for 4-2, he promptly lost his serve. At deuce, instead of punching away a volley, he tried to place the ball. This, though, offered Zib time to dash forward to earn a break point with a simple pass. That was followed by a double fault.

There were times when Henman could be heard chuntering in frustration over the failings of his first serve and, towards the end of the second set and early in the third, his first-serve percentage had fallen to 45 per cent, instead of the 65 or plus that he would have wished, especially on grass. Henman admitted that he had 'probably stayed back a bit too much' on his second serve and that was undoubtedly true. When he was playing freely and positively he looked almost as good as ever, such as when he finished with three aces and a service winner.

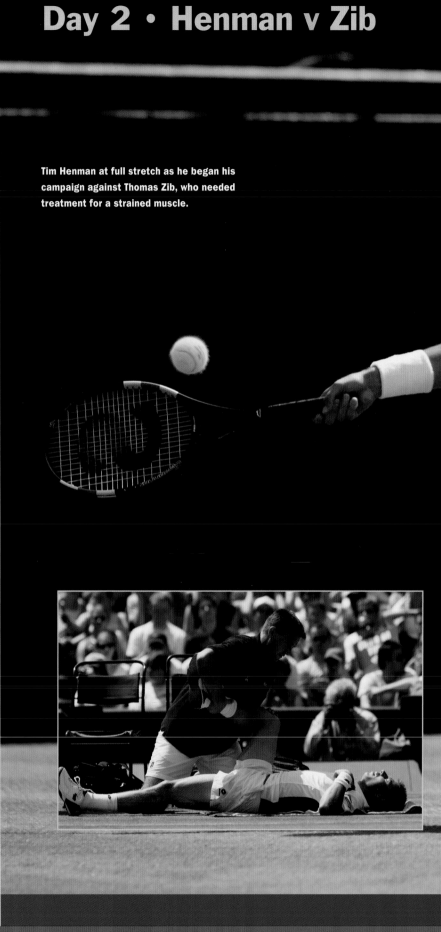

Tim Henman at full stretch as he began his campaign against Thomas Zib, who needed treatment for a strained muscle.

Jamie Delgado (below) raised British spirits by taking a set from Andre Agassi (right) while Olivier Rochus (top right) floored seventh-seeded Guillermo Coria.

Bottom, far right: Britain's Elena Baltacha's ponytail, as well as the ball, went flying as she took a set from Jelena Dokic.

• Baltacha v Dokic

Elsewhere on the British front, there was little encouragement with defeats for wild cards, Jamie Delgado, Mark Hilton, Richard Broomfield, Martin Lee and Alex Bogdanovic although the diminutive Delgado at least had the spirited compensation of deservedly taking a set off second-seeded, world number one, Andre Agassi. The 1992 champion had earned £16m in prize money during his career, 81 times as much as the 26-year-old, ranked 458, but the way Delgado rebounded from losing the second set 6-0 to hit a host of flashing winners in taking the third made it an honourable challenge. Not that Agassi seemed perturbed. Finding his range well enough for him in later rounds was what mattered most to the veteran American after his 6-4, 6-0, 5-7, 6-4 victory.

Life had not been easy for Kiev-born Elena Baltacha since she beat the seeded Amanda Coetzer to reach the third round a year earlier and there was more disappointment for her when she went agonisingly close to capturing the even more prestigious scalp of Jelena Dokic this time. Baltacha, still not entirely clear from the liver damage first diagnosed in September 2002, suddenly folded on her own serve after being within two points at 4-3 of being guaranteed the chance to serve for the match. She was broken to love in the ninth game, after earlier matching Dokic in several thrilling, high-powered rallies but was unable to prevent British interest in the ladies' singles ending completely in the first round for the first time, losing 6-3, 1-6, 6-4.

Although six of his fellow countrymen had already suffered first-round defeats, David Nalbandian was convinced that he could still make at least as significant a mark as in 2002, when he became the first South American finalist since Alex Olmedo became champion, in 1959. 'If I play as well as I know I can, then I think I can beat anybody' he forecast after his 7-5, 6-4, 6-2 defeat of Vladimir Voltchkov, who was not only struggling with loss of form but also injury.

Another Argentine, 7th-seeded Guillermo Coria, who beat Agassi at the French Open before losing to Martin Verkerk, was beaten in straight sets by Belgium's Olivier Rochus, at 5ft 5in, the shortest player in the draw. Rochus's 7-5, 7-6 (7-4), 6-3 success helped

Plain sailing for David Nalbandian (above) as he beat Vladimir Voltchkov but the plot went horribly wrong for Xavier Malisse (above right) as he slumped to defeat against French qualifier, Cyril Saulnier. Raemon Sluiter (far right) won a late-night thriller against Yevgeny Kafelnikov and Juan Carlos Ferrero (right) easily dismissed Jean-Rene Lisnard (below).

to compensate Belgium for the earlier than ex-pected defeat of the previous year's semi-final-ist, Xavier Malisse, who did not exactly freeze but was clearly feeling the pressure of having so many points to defend from 12 months ear-lier and was well beaten 6-4, 6-3, 6-2 by the king of French qualifiers, Cyril Saulnier.

Although this was the first time he had made it into the Wimbledon draw in three at-tempts, it was the 13th time in two years that Saulnier, 27, had fought his way through qualifying into a tournament.

Juan Carlos Ferrero, the French Open champion, who two years earlier had lost on his Wimbledon debut to Greg Rusedski in the third round, lost his serve to trail 1-2 in the opening set against Frenchman, Jean-Rene Lis-nard, but immediately broke back and there-after impressed the Centre Court crowd with his stylish shot-making to win 6-2, 6-1, 6-3.

For 24-year-old, 6ft 5in Dutchman, Verk-erk, however, the unseeded runner-up at Roland Garros, there was no dream Wimble-don debut. Playing only the second match of his career on grass, he had earlier played down the possible impact of his ferocious serves and brilliant returns by saying 'I'm not very good at bending low, which you have to do a lot on this surface'. He was right. His 6-3, 6-4, 6-7 (5-7), 6-1 defeat by Swedish qualifier, Robin Soderling, bore out his apprehension.

The attendance of 41,929 set a record for Day Two of The Championships, and many of them stayed late into the evening to admire a high-quality struggle in which Verkerk's com-patriot, Raemon Sluiter outgunned Yevgeny Kafelnikov, 7-5, 3-6, 2-6, 6-2, 6-3. It finished at 8.55 pm. Earlier in a match suspended by fading light on Monday, 15th-seeded French-man, Arnaud Clement, completed a battling 6-3, 4-6, 7-6 (7-2), 6-7 (3-7), 10-8 victory over American newcomer, Robby Ginepri, who saved six match points before succumbing after 4 hours 33 minutes.

Those who felt that after the shock for Hewitt even Serena Williams might have felt vulnerable when she opened the defence of the ladies' singles title — especially having had the French Open crown taken from her — were swiftly disabused. Although she lost concentration early in the second set against

Harkleroad

a 5ft 3in opponent, Jill Craybas, who was no Karlovic, Williams closed out a 6-3, 6-3 success and was clearly delighted to be offered an affectionate ovation after the French jeers and boos that marked her last departure from a court.

Justine Henin-Hardenne, the 2001 finalist, had her left wrist and two fingers bandaged following a fall a week earlier, as she set about trying to add the Wimbledon title to her triumph at Roland Garros. She saved two break points at 2-2 in a first set she took 7-5, but romped away with the second 6-1 against Julia Vakulenko.

Meanwhile, Jennifer Capriati, who needed just 19 minutes to sweep through the first set, when her forehand was firing at full power, took only another 23 to complete an impressive 6-1, 6-3 victory over Switzerland's Myriam Casanova.

With the top seeds in such easy command, the day's greatest impact among the ladies was made by the recently-turned-16 Maria Sharapova, as she emphatically dismissed the 18-year-old leading American hope, Ashley Harkleroad, 6-2, 6-1.

'I was getting my clock cleaned out there' said Harkleroad. She was also treated to those high-decibel shrieks and squeals that Sharapova seems to utter almost every time she strikes the ball — except, oddly enough, when practising. That and the constant thigh-slapping that would not have been out of place in a chorus line, certainly enlivened the day on Court Two, as did the noisy court-side urging from her father, Yuri.

The ladies' singles gained pace once defending champion, Serena Williams, opened the Centre Court programme against Jill Craybas. Jennifer Capriati (above) was little troubled by Miriam Casanova but (below left) Russian junior, Miriam Sharapova, surprised the talented American, Ashley Harkleroad.

WEDNESDAY 25 JUNE

Day 3

Greg Rusedski (above) was handling the Andy Roddick serve well enough until a rogue call from the crowd led to his major altercations with umpire Lars Graff — and his downfall.

Everyone was expecting something special when Greg Rusedski and Andy Roddick, the joint holders of the world's fastest serving record (149 mph) walked onto Centre Court to challenge one another in a potentially ferocious shoot-out in the second round.

No one, though, had predicted just how explosive the climax would be. Rusedski, poised, it seemed, to take the third set after losing the first two in tie-breaks, completely lost his self-control after a rogue cry of 'out', from someone in the crowd, prompted him to pause following his initial return.

The British number two was 5-2 up in the third when an excited spectator made his disastrous intervention believing that Roddick's shot had dropped beyond the baseline. Rusedski, after a fractional pause, played on but so did Roddick, so the Swedish umpire, Lars Graff, gave Roddick the point. For the next couple of minutes or so the air, not only in the arena but all round the world on television, was blue as Rusedski expressed his feelings in such uncouth terms that Barry Davies, the BBC TV commentator, felt obliged to apologise to viewers on the British player's behalf.

Many felt that the point should have been replayed, but the umpire applied the Rules of Tennis correctly, as referee Alan Mills pointed out a day later when Rusedski, who had been beaten 7-6 (7-4), 7-6 (7-1), 7-5 was fined £1,500 for uttering an audible obscenity.

As Rusedski admitted, a player with his experience should have been professional enough to cast the burning fury from his mind, still win the third set and fight to continue the comeback he had started. Instead he threw it all away. He was broken to love when serving at 5-3 and then launched another ferocious verbal attack on the match official in what became a classic example of self-destruction.

'I wanted it so badly and then lost it a little bit' he said with huge understatement. 'I didn't handle it the best I could and I regret it. For people who were offended, I apologise.'

In a way what happened was understandable, albeit unforgivable. After so long in hibernation because of injuries, Rusedski had been playing by far the most competitive, consistent and intense tennis of the summer in the first two sets. He might have won the tie-break at

the end of the opening set but a slightly mishit forehand gave Roddick the key mini-break for 5-3 in the first of them and then an unforced error on the first point of the second tie-break left the American racing through it 7-1.

All this and a couple of net cords that went Roddick's way contributed to Rusedski's frustration and the eruption that left him with no realistic hope of avenging his defeat by the feisty 20-year-old American at Queen's Club two weeks earlier.

Away from Rusedski's notorious fall from grace, four more men's seeds were beaten but one of the more significant aspects of the day was Roger Federer's easy passage into the third round. After what had happened to him a year earlier, Federer knew it was vital for him to build confidence throughout the first week and there was more than enough evidence of that in his 7-5, 6-1, 6-1 defeat of Austrian, Stefan Koubek, to suggest that his game was starting nicely to fall into place.

He knew he was lucky to win the first set. Koubek led 5-2 but the match then took a dramatic turn against him when he missed an easy forehand volley while serving at 5-3, 30-15. Federer capitalised ruthlessly and took complete charge, winning 17 of the last 19 games and then looked forward to being challenged 48 hours later by Mardy Fish, who

had dismissed fellow American, Jan-Michael Gambill 6-4, 6-4, 6-1.

At the other end of the age scale, Todd Martin, fast approaching his 33rd birthday, demonstrated that he could still remain a threat on grass by beating 17th-seeded Gustavo Kuerten, 7-6 (7-4), 6-4, 6-4. Had Wimbledon still been able to seed almost solely on grass-court form and past performances, rather than restrict the seeding to the 32-highest-ranked players, Martin, a 1996 semi-finalist, might still have been on the list.

The first set was the key when Martin hit three aces in the opening game and was always in the driving seat after the three-times former French champion double-faulted on the first point of the tie-break. He repeated the error to be broken in the third game of the second set, whereas Martin's serve held firm throughout.

South Americans overall continued to struggle, with two more Argentine seeds, Augustin Calleri and Juan Ignacio Chela losing respectively to Brazil's Flavio Saretta and Romanian Victor Hanescu, but Thailand's engaging Paradorn Srichaphan was smiling again. He had been struggling in the first half of the year but rediscovered the exciting form which proved too much for Andre Agassi at Wimbledon a year earlier and provided him the springboard for an outstanding second

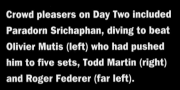
Crowd pleasers on Day Two included Paradorn Srichaphan, diving to beat Olivier Mutis (left) who had pushed him to five sets, Todd Martin (right) and Roger Federer (far left).

Rafael Nadal (left) had too much clout for Britain's Lee Childs (top left). Stefan Koubek (above) was under pressure from Roger Federer on a day when Rainer Schuettler (above right) and Sjeng Schalken (below left) also made progress.

half of 2002. He was clearly overjoyed by the way he had survived a traumatic contest with Olivier Mutis, eventually winning 4-6, 1-6, 7-6 (7-4), 7-5, 7-5 after breaking back when the Frenchman was serving for the match at 5-4 in the fourth set.

The first rain of The Championships could not have arrived at a worse time for Britain's Lee Childs, the only one among Britain's 14 wild cards to have survived the first round. To his credit, though, he did not offer that as more than a contributory irritation in his 6-2, 6-4, 6-3 defeat by the prodigiously gifted Spanish teenager, Rafael Nadal.

'I made too many mistakes. I wasn't solid enough from the start,' Childs admitted after the first set had slipped away from him so comprehensively that even a group of spectators wrapped in the flags of St George decided he was a lost cause. Had they shown him rather more loyalty, Childs would have rewarded them with a far more resilient display in the second set. Indeed, but for one glaring volley error at 5-4, he might have won it.

At the start of the third set, Childs produced a couple of spectacular forehands to break Nadal and the initiative was still very much

with him when the drizzle sent them back to the locker room after 52 minutes. When they resumed, the British player's hopes evaporated rapidly. He was passed on the first point, double-faulted on the second, shanked a forehand to 15-40 and then sent a backhand wide and did not win another game.

The focus of the day in the ladies' singles was on Daniela Hantuchova, the Slovakian, whose many supporters were alternating between admiring her tennis and worrying about her beanstalk frame. It was another emotional day for the ninth seed for although number one in the list of photographic pin-up targets, especially in the injury absence of Anna Kournikova, she slumped to an embarrassing and tearful exit against the modest Japanese player, Shinobu Asagoe.

All seemed well as Hantuchova dictated every game in the first set but bizarrely, two hours later, she was beaten in a thrilling 2-hour-47-minute struggle on Court Two, during which she amassed more than 50 unforced errors. Asagoe, ranked 78 and a finalist at Edgbaston two weeks earlier, had fought off three match points in the ninth and tenth games of an almost wildly erratic final set in which she also failed to serve out for the match at 8-7. When the chance to do so came a second time, her nerve held for a 0-6, 6-4, 12-10 triumph.

Asked why she more than once shed tears on court in the closing stages, Hantuchova said 'This tournament means so much to me. I'll have to work hard on the mental side of my game because I've been in this position several times before and lost. I have to start taking my chances.'

Hantuchova was the highest of the four seeds beaten in the ladies' event. She followed 17th-ranked Amanda Coetzer, who was outlasted 4-6, 7-5, 6-4 by Italy's Francesca Schiavone, the Czech Republic's 30th-seeded Denisa Chladkova was upset by Zimbabwe's Cara Black, 6-2, 6-3, and Spain's 24th-seeded Magui Serna was beaten by Slovenia's Marta Matevzic 7-6, 2-6, 6-4.

Those tipped to last longest were largely untroubled, with Venus Williams, Kim Clijsters and Lindsay Davenport dropping only 13 second-round games between them in six sets.

Lleyton Hewitt lent his support unobtrusively to girlfriend, Kim Clijsters (right), as she beat Virginie Razzano, while in one of the surprises of the day, the overjoyed Shinobu Asagoe celebrated victory over Daniela Hantuchova (bottom left). Venus Williams (left) was serene against Katarina Srebotnik.

THE CHAMPIONSHIPS
WIMBLEDON

THURSDAY 26 JUNE

Day 4

For more than a century, tennis players from all nations have dreamed of becoming a champion on Centre Court. For the talented few, it becomes reality. For the majority it remains a tantalising fantasy although Hollywood wants to make everyone believe it can come true.

That is the story the makers of 'Four Weddings and a Funeral', 'Bridget Jones's Diary' and 'Billy Elliot' were creating, for a film simply entitled 'Wimbledon', due for release in the autumn of 2004.

For nearly an hour before Tim Henman arrived, half an hour later than the normal start time, to continue his quest to bring a personal lifelong ambition to fruition, the crowd found themselves as movie extras, cheering 'Peter Colt', a fictional 31-year-old British player with a wild card, walking on court to begin what might just prove to have been the final. The film makers were being cagey about what round it would be although, being a romantic drama, there must surely be a happy ending.

The overture to the day's play was make-believe. Henman against the French qualifier, Michael Llodra, was for real. Maybe it also helped Henman for his performance showed a marked improvement on his form in the first round. He, though, was guarded and, although rightfully happy to have lifted his game so swiftly for a 6-4, 6-4, 6-3 win, said:

'Hopefully it was not a reflection on our desperation to try and win this tournament one day that they have to make a film about it.'

One suggestion was that instead of 'Wimbledon' the new film should be called 'Home Alone 2' but Henman offered a more practical and defiant response, saying 'We've got to break out of the run we're in. It's been too long with the standard as poor as it's been.'

Then to underline his lasting ability to provide the inspiration for others to follow, Henman sharpened his game when it was most needed, at 5-4 in the opening set, at which he broke to 15 helped by biting returns after saving two break points at 2-2 and again when the left-handed Frenchman was serving at 4-5 in the second set. This time he pounded glorious angled winners into the corners, two on the backhand and one on the

forehand before completing the second set with another unreturnable forehand.

Henman suffered a blip early in the third set when he double-faulted on the first point, again to 15-40 and also offered Llodra two more opportunities after working his way back to deuce. 'Allez' cried Llodra, when he at last took his chance with a whipped backhand cross-court return but, urged on by cries of 'C'mon Tiger', the British number one broke back immediately. Two games later Henman produced a perfect lob to break again and, as in the first round, kept his best for last, holding his last two service games to love and finishing with a serve-and-volley drive that illustrated the benefit of his added aggression.

For much of Day Four, Number One Court was the place to be, not least when David Nalbandian, Henman's next challenger, maintained his progress with a 6-2, 7-5, 6-2 win over Andre Sa, the Brazilian who had reached the last eight a year earlier. It was alluring, as

Andre Sa (below) who was unable to halt David Nalbandian.

Asked if he felt fortunate that he had been drawn against a lucky loser in the first round followed by a qualifier in both the second and third rounds, Tim Henman, who had just quipped that sometimes he even got blamed for the weather when it rains at Wimbledon, replied 'Am I also going to get blamed for picking them out as well?'

well as potentially threatening for British hopes, to see Nalbandian, the last survivor from the nine Argentines who set out on the Wimbledon journey, moving ever more naturally to the net to put away volleys when the opportunity was offered.

The centrepiece of the Number One Court programme had started the day when Andre Agassi, convinced he could repeat his title triumph from 11 years earlier, beat Lars Burgsmuller 6-3, 7-6 (7-4), 6-3 without ever once coming to the net behind either a first or second serve. He did not need to do so. The sight of the venerable American skilfully directing operations from the back of the court is like watching a coaching masterclass. There were times when it seemed as if he had a noose round the German's neck, running and pulling him to submission.

To his credit, Burgsmuller kept searching for ways to pierce Agassi's defence and resolve but could never do so enough or at the right times to make more than a dent in a generally sleek Agassi performance. One felt for the German. At least three times in the early stages he struck shots that could have been spectacular winners in most instances, only for Agassi, always perfectly positioned, to take one quick step and return in even more devastating fashion.

Next up for Agassi would be the Moroccan, Younes El Aynaoui, a 7-6 (7-5), 3-6, 7-6 (7-4), 6-4 winner over Chile's Nicolas Massu but also hovering menacingly still, in the bottom half of the draw, was the unseeded Australian, Mark Philippoussis. He beat French qualifier, Cyril Saulnier, 6-3, 6-2, 7-6 (7-2), and there were 19 aces from a player who had reached the last eight three times in succession between 1998 and 2000, before a serious injury, after he had brilliantly taken a first set from Pete Sampras, left his career in the balance.

While Philippoussis was honing his serves, volleys and thunderous forehands on Number Three Court, James Blake, seriously short of match practice after injuring his right shoulder at Queen's Club, was becoming the only men's casualty of the day on Court Number Two. The 26th-seeded American Davis Cup player, with a British passport — his mother hails from Banbury — delivered an alarming number of loose shots against the Armenian, Sargis Sargsian and was beaten 6-2, 7-6 (7-3), 6-2 in under two hours.

Juan Carlos Ferrero lost the opening set against Nicolas Escude but found himself through to the last 32 quicker than expected when the Frenchman, who lost the second set and had needed an injection to ease the pain

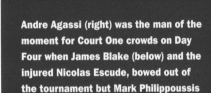

Andre Agassi (right) was the man of the moment for Court One crowds on Day Four when James Blake (below) and the injured Nicolas Escude, bowed out of the tournament but Mark Philippoussis (bottom left) began to make his move.

Winners all in round two, Serena Williams, who fended off a worthy challenge by Els Callens, Jennifer Capriati (top right) and Jelena Dokic.

A busy day for some of the leading ladies. Mary Pierce (above) on the way to beating the seeded Eleni Daniilidou, then clockwise, Justine Henin-Hardenne beating Flavia Pennetta, seen below her, Lina Krasnoroutskaya, who was unable to resist the pressure from fellow Russian, Anastasia Myskina (far right) and the photogenic Maria Sharapova who upset Elena Bovina in another all-Russian contest.

from an injured hip before the tournament began, twice fell during the third set and decided to retire.

For once during the first week of a Grand Slam, there were occasionally tricky though not seriously turbulent waters for the leading ladies, including Serena Williams and Justine Henin-Hardenne even though both they and Jennifer Capriati all won in straight sets with varying degrees of difficulty.

Capriati, with her hefty serving always to the fore, enjoyed the most comprehensive success, taking only 47 minutes to dismiss her Swiss rival, Marie-Gaianeh Mikaelian, 6-2, 6-1, especially as her 38th-ranked opponent double-faulted too often for her own good.

Serena Williams should not have been surprised by the tough fight she faced from the least known of the challenging Belgians, Els Callens, who had taken the eventual champion to two tie-breaks 12 months earlier. The Callens strategy was clear. She was

determined to try and move Serena around enough to force her into errors, just as she had done in 2002. It did not work in the first set, especially after the American broke for 3-2 and the second set looked like being a disaster for Callens's confidence when she found herself 0-4 under the sheer weight of the Williams serve and groundstrokes.

Yet at 1-4 she at last managed to draw the defending champion into dangerous mid-court territory and start passing her or making her overhit from the baseline. Suddenly it was 4-4 and everyone was paying attention. Yet having been run ragged in failing to save a break point in that eighth game, Williams decided it was time to get serious. In the next game she earned another break point of her own with a heavily hammered forehand and exaggerated shout to match — and strode on to a 6-4, 6-4 victory.

Henin-Hardenne kept the Belgian flag flying but only after a torrid first set as she struggled to combat the spectacular double-fisted backhand blows from the 21-year-old Italian, Flavia Pennetta. It provided rich entertainment although ultimately Pennetta, making her Wimbledon debut, lost the first set 7-6 (7-2) and partly beat herself when her serve let her down in a 6-1 second set.

If the first Tuesday still retains some semblance of being Ladies' Day at The Championships, there were seven good reasons for this to have been called 'Russia's Day'. At a time when they seem to have a conveyor belt of talented girls making headway, three starred on Court 3, two on Court 18 and two more on Courts 13 and 5 respectively.

On a day when Mary Pierce, 28, was also trying to revive memories of her tennis at the top by upsetting 14th-seeded, Eleni Daniilidou 6-4, 6-1, four of the new generation of Russians accompanied her in joining Vera Zvonareva and Nadia Petrova, two other Russians already in the third round. Anastasia Myskina won at the expense of compatriot, Lina Krasnoroutskaya; Svetlana Kuznetsova, who like Marat Safin developed her game in Spain, beat the South Korean, Yoon Jeong Cho; Elena Dementieva beat Spaniard, Arantxa Parra; and most prominently of all, Maria Sharapova, 16, beat Elena Bovina, 20. Sharapova, only slightly noisier but hitting with considerably more power than her rival, won what Andrew Baker of The Daily Telegraph called 'the battle of the Russian dolls' 6-3, 6-1.

THE CHAMPIONSHIPS WIMBLEDON

FRIDAY 27 JUNE

Day 5

On a day when the leading contenders in both the men's and ladies' singles progressed nicely, with only one of the seeds losing to a lower-ranked opponent, it was a chance to concentrate on a few other protagonists who had already created upsets or might be challenging for glory in the years ahead. A stroll along St Mary's Walk, past the ever-full Henman Hill to Number One Court was a good place to start for there, Rafael Nadal, 17, the youngest player in the men's singles, was pitting his heavy-hitting wits and speed about the court against the extra experience and guile of Paradorn Srichaphan from Thailand.

Nadal's victories over Mario Ancic and Lee Childs had already sent some Spanish journalists into a frenzy of exaggerated excitement. 'He's the most likely Spaniard to win Wimbledon since Manuel Santana in 1966' one of them trumpeted, before adding 'And wouldn't it be great if he could win this year and replace Boris Becker, who was also 17 when he won in 1985, as the youngest champion?'

Well maybe. It might even have also provided the Hollywood film-makers with a sub-plot for their story but it was clearly asking too much of this precociously gifted user of power and spin who, after all, was only playing his second tournament on grass. The first had been 12 months earlier when he reached the semi-finals of the junior boys' singles, whereas Srichaphan had effectively made himself known at The Championships in 2002 by knocking out Andre Agassi.

Not surprisingly, therefore, although Nadal charged round the court as if practising to be a matador, his limitations were fully exposed as he was beaten 6-4, 6-4, 6-2 by Srichaphan's superior all-round qualities. 'If I want to win more matches I have to develop my serve' said Nadal, who had seen first and second serves either picked off at will by his opponent or returned in such a way that he was lured into positions that allowed Srichaphan to deliver a telling pass.

The opening game was a case in point. Someone had clearly advised Nadal that on grass you need to get to the net as quickly as possible when serving to put away volleys.

Fine when the moment is right but on the first two points Nadal found himself diving forlornly to try and counter brilliant returns.

At 0-30 he stayed back but was just as haplessly drawn in and passed during the rally. Nadal is a quick learner when things go wrong and could well be a serious threat by the time Wimbledon 2004 arrives, but on this afternoon Srichaphan enjoyed his role as the tutor.

Paradorn Srichaphan (opposite) was too experienced for Spanish teenager, Rafael Nadal.

Opposite page, clockwise from the top: Jonas Bjorkman, Justin Gimelstob, who lost to the Swede, Sjeng Schalken, a straight-sets winner into the third round and Todd Martin, whose 11th Wimbledon was brought to an end by Rainer Schuettler.

Below: Andy Roddick in action while wearing down a stubborn Tommy Robredo.

Out on Court 13, Ivo Karlovic, the 6ft 10in giant who had performed the tournament's first giant-killing act at the expense of defending champion, Lleyton Hewitt, found himself slain by the hardly diminutive 6ft 5in Max Mirnyi, the 1998 mixed doubles champion with Serena Williams, unkindly dubbed 'The Beast of Belarus.'

Needless to say it was serve-dominated. More than 50 per cent of the points were settled by a serve alone and there were only six break points in the four sets before Mirnyi became the first Belarusian to reach the last 16 with a 7-6 (7-5), 3-6, 6-3, 7-6 (7-4) victory. Karlovic hit another 26 aces, bringing his total from three qualifying matches and three in the main draw to 154. He will never forget his first Grand Slam or that Centre Court day in the sun when he became part of tennis history.

The long and short of it was that, although Karlovic outscored Mirnyi 70-43 in aces and other winners, he also missed a few too many of his limited chances, including a break point

that would have allowed him to serve for the fourth set.

Once again the veteran Todd Martin became ensnared in a marathon, though this time his steadfast determination and wily strategy failed to prevail. He was beaten 4-6, 7-5, 6-7 (1-7), 6-1, 7-5 in three and a half hours by Rainer Schuettler, the German ninth seed. Despite slumping to 0-5 in the fourth set, the American did not surrender. Anything but; it would not have been in his nature to do so. Even after being broken at 4-4 in the final set he immediately broke back, only for the Australian Open runner-up to break once more to 6-5 helped by a net cord that dribbled over on the first point.

Sweden's Jonas Bjorkman, 31, still enjoying himself as much in singles as the doubles, where he and Todd Woodbridge were defending the men's title, struck an extra blow for longevity in the game by outclassing the American, Justin Gimelstob, five years his junior, 6-1, 6-3, 6-3 while Holland's Sjeng Schalken, another perennial dangerous floater, again applied his rasping serve effectively to beat the Romanian, Victor Hanescu.

As for the remaining top-ranked men on display, Roger Federer and Andy Roddick continued to progress towards a likely semi-final showdown that would be eagerly awaited. While Federer was warming up on Centre Court against Mardy Fish, the 45th-ranked, fast-improving American, who had reached the Nottingham final on grass less than a week earlier, someone raised a banner in the crowd that read 'Sampras, we miss you.'

True enough. Not only Wimbledon but the game generally was missing him although to a certain extent in this match and then most emphatically in the final days of the tournament, the 21-year-old from Basle would be doing his bit to underline the adage 'The King is Dead, Long Live the King.'

Federer looked in total command by the time light drizzle interrupted play for a while but at 4-4 in the third he experienced one of those wobbles that had raised question marks about his temperament on the big occasion. This time, though, he snapped straight back into form, before there was the chance for his shoulders to droop or the uncertainty to creep into his mind.

Though far from satisfied by the way he occasionally struggled to cope with the pace and power of Tommy Robredo's groundstrokes in the first set, Roddick thrilled the Centre Court crowd as he went on to stamp his authority comprehensively for a 7-6 (7-5), 6-4, 6-4 win.

When he took a toilet break at the end of the first set, in which he faced his only break point, Roddick was shaking his head with obvious frustration. He still did not look entirely content with his form in the early stages of the second but in the third his control was complete. The declining number of points he lost on serve emphasised his command. They reduced from 11 in the first set to nine in the second and only five in the third.

The only disappointment among the crowd was that his fastest serve was a mere 134 mph, against his Queen's Club record of 149 mph. Not that he minded. 'The speed is irrelevant, it's how effective the serve is that matters' he said, wisely.

The possibility that Venus Williams might face her first serious test of the fortnight against Nadia Petrova, the 5ft 10in young Russian, who had beaten Jennifer Capriati in Paris, was grossly unfounded. Although Petrova demonstrated that she could strike 100 mph-plus serves and volley with ease on both flanks, she was too often overcome, it seemed, by the occasion. She double-faulted to lose the first set and suffered the same embarrassment on match point, allowing the former champion to coast through to a 6-1, 6-2 victory in 62 minutes.

At least, though, it boosted Williams's confidence for her fourth-round bid to avenge her French Open defeat by another Russian prodigy, Vera Zvonareva, who also completed the first week without dropping a set by beating Uzbekistan's Iroda Tulyaganova, 6-3, 7-5.

It was another easy day too for Kim Clijsters, who outplayed the American, Samantha Reeves, 6-1, 6-2. Clijsters romped away with the first five games in only 20 minutes but after dropping only seven games in three matches, knew there were tougher tasks ahead, not least in the next round against her

doubles partner, Ai Sugiyama, who won their last singles clash in February.

Lindsay Davenport, seeded to meet Venus Williams in the quarter-finals, was surprised by Petrova's capitulation against the fourth seed but had carried out an effective demolition job of her own against Zimbabwe's Cara Black, 6-2, 6-2.

The only seeding upset to raise an eyebrow came when Chanda Rubin found the Italian, Silvia Farina Elia in inspired form as she won her rain-interrupted contest on Number One Court, 7-6 (8-6), 6-3.

Opposite page, top left: Vera Zvonareva was secure from the back of the court in beating Iroda Tulyaganova, while Silvia Farina Elia celebrated victory over Chanda Rubin, pictured above her.

By now the doubles events were also in full swing, with much of the attention once more concentrated on Martina Navratilova and her two chances in the ladies' doubles and mixed doubles of equalling Billie Jean's record of 20 Wimbledon titles. Navratilova, a young-at-heart 46, helped her partner, Svetlana Kuznetsova, celebrate her 18th birthday, 6-2, 6-1 at the expense of Britain's Helen Crook and Anna Hawkins, who nevertheless went home proudly recalling their impressive first-round success over Barbara Schett and Patty Schnyder.

When Martina Navratilova (seen above with doubles partner, Svetlana Kuznetsova) first played at Wimbledon in 1973, as a 16-year-old, her first-round opponent in the ladies' singles was Christine Truman. 'I didn't know anything about her so I asked around the locker room,' the former runner-up recalls. 'Oh, isn't she that young Czech everyone's talking about' someone told her. 30 years on everyone was still talking about her.

Overnight campers no doubt dreamt of a
Saturday spot on Centre Court (inset)
under sunny skies.

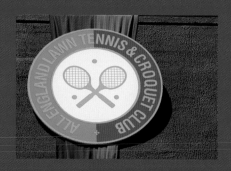

Former Test umpire, Dickie Bird, and Newcastle United and former England manager, Sir Bobby Robson, were in the Royal Box to watch Tim Henman (right) beat Swedish teenager, Robin Soderling, after David Nalbandian (top far right) had recovered from two sets down to beat the lunging Karol Kucera.

Kucera

It had been a long, patient wait — mainly because Andre Agassi and Younes El Aynaoui had earlier delighted the Centre Court for more than three hours in a masterly contest — but in the end Tim Henman and his fans were well rewarded.

Playing his sharpest, most positive tennis of the first week, the British hero took only 1 hour 34 minutes to swoop into the last 16 for the eighth year in succession with a 6-3, 6-1 6-4 victory over the 18-year-old Swedish qualifier, Robin Soderling.

By doing so, he had taken full advantage of a benevolent draw — a wild card, followed by a qualifier in the second and third rounds — that had dropped into his lap and was able to look ahead to the tougher challenges ahead, with growing confidence.

In Grand Slam tournaments, more than any other, no match can be taken for granted. Indeed one reason why seeds have to be especially wary of qualifiers is that they have already accustomed themselves to playing on grass by winning three matches the week before at Roehampton, a task that many regard as almost as tense and nerve-wracking as The Championships themselves.

He started briskly against a clearly apprehensive Soderling and with the exception of a minor wobble in the third set, when he was broken while serving for the match at 5-2, generally displayed that aggressive, well-controlled authority which had not always been evident in the weeks leading into The Championships.

Soderling's double fault on the first point of his opening service game did not help the youngster's prospects although the firmly struck groundstrokes that earned him one chance to break back in the game that followed, suggested that Henman would have to work for his victory. Long before the end of a reasonably close first set, it was clear that Henman was serve-and-volleying with a refreshing, new-found freedom and, more importantly, it was paying off. He scampered through the second set in 21 minutes and had three chances to break for 5-3 in the third before the temporary hiccup.

Henman's contented mood, as he looked forward to a fourth-round meeting with David Nalbandian, was reflected in his opinion that he was 'very happy with the way I'm serving. It has come a hell of a long way since Queen's. My whole game is moving in the right direction even though, on the other side of the coin, I know I haven't played so much as I would have liked. I hope that isn't going to have any bearing on the second week.'

There was another reason why the British hero had reason to be cheerful. Even with his late start he had finished before Nalbandian had completed the four-and-a-half-hour task of wearing down the Slovakian, Karol Kucera on Number One Court, 6-4, 5-7, 6-7 (1-7), 6-4, 6-2. It was a match in which quantity was more evident than quality, with little consistency from either player on serves or returns, so that the crowd only became excited in the closing games of the final set.

When Nalbandian led by a set and 4-1, it looked as if he would win in a canter but his serve then fell apart and in the end it was Kucera after treatment for an ankle injury in the third set, who was left reflecting on what might have been. Not only had he worked his way back to win the second set but taken the third in a 7-1 tie-break before also leading 2-1 in the fifth with five chances to break for 3-1, only to squander four of them with unforced errors.

There was no doubt that the most compelling tennis of the day came from Agassi and El Aynaoui in their delightfully entertaining and competitive Centre Court match that the oldest man in the draw was to win 5-7, 6-4, 7-6 (7-4), 7-6 (7-4). Agassi had won all four of their previous encounters but this was their first on grass and one of their best, enthralling not only the tennis cognoscenti but other sporting giants in the Royal Box, including Sir Bobby Robson, rowing stars, Sir Stephen Redgrave, Matthew Pinsent and James Cracknell plus Jason Leonard, Lawrence Delaglio and Johnny Wilkinson from England's triumphant Rugby team.

One loose game by Agassi allowed El Aynaoui to serve out for the first set in the 12th game but suddenly, after the second set also went with serve, he had the Moroccan racing back and forth as he broke to level the match in the tenth game. The points were crisp and accurate, the rallies often long and tantalising with little to choose between them until the third-set tie-break when El Aynaoui's concentration briefly but expensively wavered.

The drama continued in the fourth when El Aynaoui, leading 5-4, had Agassi at 0-40 but in typical fashion he clawed, scratched and fought his way out of trouble and went on to win the tie-break and the match. 'I had four chances to break at 4-4 and he got through the game so it was up to me to do the same when I was in trouble' said Agassi, who would go on to face the big-serving Australian, Mark Philippoussis, after a day's rest on the Sunday.

For the first time in 12 years Philippoussis found himself in the same boat as Henman, his country's lone survivor in the third round and he made sure of staying alive with a 4-6, 7-6 (9-7), 6-4, 7-6 (8-6), defeat of the 35th seed, Radek Stepanek from the Czech Republic. His start was shaky. He double-faulted twice and was passed twice and Stepanek held on to the advantage for the rest of the set. In the second set, however, the Philippoussis serve began to find the range he needed but it was only after a sixth game of 11 deuces, in which he had two break points, and a 1-4 deficit in the tie-break that he started to shine with six consecutive points to draw level. By comparison the rest was a sprint with the Philippoussis ace tally steadily climbing towards an impressive total of 33.

In a week that had been notable for successes by some of the tallest men in the game, the pint-sized Belgian, Olivier Rochus, stood tall at 5ft 5in after beating Jarkko Nieminen, the first player from Finland to be seeded (30) at The Championships, 7-6 (7-5), 6-3, 6-1. It was a strange contest. Nieminen led 3-0 in the first set but then lost his way and did not appear to be totally committed to finding it again. Having beaten an opponent only six inches taller, however, Rochus knew he would have an even more daunting task 48 hours later against Germany's 6ft 7in Alexander Popp in what would be an even more obvious little and large show.

Towards the end of a first week in which the leading ladies had generally won

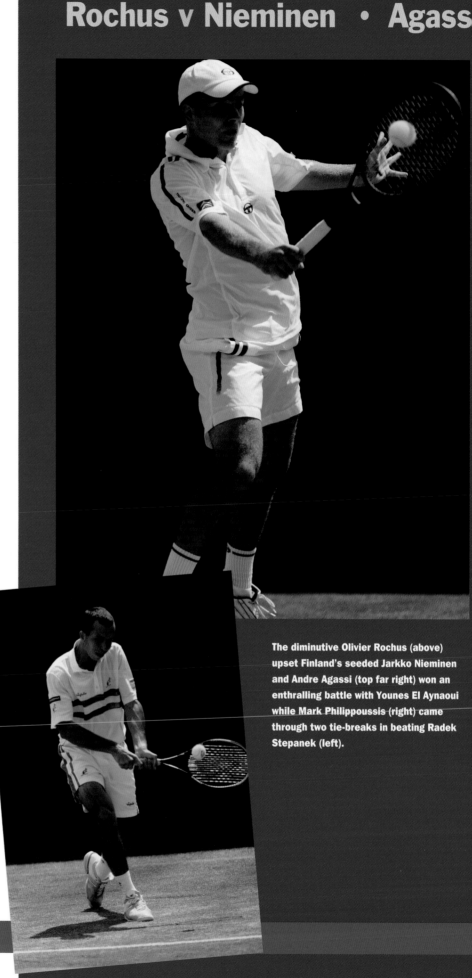

The diminutive Olivier Rochus (above) upset Finland's seeded Jarkko Nieminen and Andre Agassi (top far right) won an enthralling battle with Younes El Aynaoui while Mark Philippoussis (right) came through two tie-breaks in beating Radek Stepanek (left).

too comfortably to attract what they would have thought was their due recognition, Serena Williams certainly proved that she was stepping up her form at the right time by overwhelming the 30th-ranked Laura Granville, also from the United States, 6-3, 6-1. By the time she was leading 4-1 in the first set, Serena had dropped only eight points but the rest of the set was a rewarding, full-blooded contest with Granville taking on her opponent's groundstroke power and more often than not matching it for accuracy and intensity.

Yet as the grunting level grew louder, Serena's power increased accordingly and in a virtuouso second-set display she repeatedly passed her opponent with hefty hitting from the baseline that had earned the point even before Granville could react.

Jennifer Capriati needed treatment for a strained shoulder on the way to her 6-4, 6-4 defeat of Japan's Akiko Morigami, while Justine Henin-Hardenne accounted for Australian Alicia Molik by the same score. Mary Pierce, who admitted that she had nearly decided to bypass Wimbledon this year because she did not think her game had been rehabilitated enough to do herself justice, clearly felt she had made the right choice after upsetting the 23rd-seeded American, Lisa Raymond, 4-6, 6-3, 7-5. 'I'm just so happy and relieved' said the Florida-based French player, working again with coach, Sven Groeneveld. 'This match meant a lot to me. I played with my heart. My game's not back to where it was so I'm having to be mentally tough and fight.'

That was also true of Maria Sharapova as the 16-year-old continued her memorable Wimbledon debut by defeating the 11th-seeded Jelena Dokic, 6-4, 6-4. It was her first appearance on a show court (Number One) but she was coolness personified — and not so noisy as usual, either. 'When I stepped on the court I was thinking "I'm not going to give her a chance today, that's it. I want to be a winner today, right here, on this court." ' She punished Dokic for a double fault in the opening game and one break of serve in the fifth game of the second set was all that was required to carry her through to an all-Russian fourth-round match against Svetlana Kuznetsova.

Serena Williams (left) ended the first week with her easiest win so far — against Laura Granville and then (overleaf) was besieged by fans for her autograph.

Jennifer Capriati (above) needed treatment for a strained shoulder before overcoming Akiko Morigami but Maria Sharapova's (right) mood was as cheerful as her tennis after she upset Jelena Dokic.

Andre Agassi in full flow.

MONDAY 30 JUNE

Day 7

Day Seven dawned grey and daunting. The forecast was anything but encouraging and by noon, when the first of the many tasty-looking fourth-round matches were due on court, the rain that had been falling intermittently most of the morning was heavier than before.

Yet 20 minutes later the clouds began to lift, the court covers were removed and by 1.15 pm, play was under way. Although the matches were interrupted for about an hour almost before they had begun, thereafter a day of great drama, excitement, upsets and ultimately British celebrations began to unfold.

By the time it was over, with only one of the scheduled eight men's and eight women's singles matches unresolved, a new men's singles champion was guaranteed, six of the top seeds in the women's singles had advanced to the last eight and — best of all from a domestic point of view — Tim Henman was through to the quarter-finals for the seventh time in eight years.

In another of those familiar but none the less captivating roller-coaster journeys on which the British number one regularly embarks, he had the Centre Court crowd on the edge of their seats, the thousands on Henman Hill roaring their fluctuating delight and despair, and millions more watching nervously at home as BBC1 cleared the decks of their normal programming.

The Centre Court clock registered 8.38 pm when, 3 hours 1 minute after Henman had struck a winning serve on the opening point, David Nalbandian knew there was no longer any hope of him repeating his achievement from the year before, in becoming the first South American men's singles finalist for 43 years, when he netted a forehand as he was facing his third match point.

As usual after such a significant step forward by Henman, the Centre Court crowd was on its feet, waving Union flags and those of St George as they showed their approval of Henman's uplifting 6-2, 6-7 (4-7), 7-5, 6-3 victory.

He, in turn, wanted to thank them. 'It's a phenomenal atmosphere to play in and much appreciated' he said after a match in which he had needed all the support he could get — mostly of course from his own

inner mental and physical strengths — to stay on course after losing his grip in the second set and then failing to sustain his three consecutive breaks of the Nalbandian serve in the third set.

'The crowd support has always been pretty incredible here' said Henman. 'But they too choose their moments. It was getting pretty late. Everyone's eager to finish the match off rather than having to come back the next day and they gave me such a lift.'

He described his form as he raced away with the first set in 32 minutes and reached 3-1 in the second as 'probably as good as it gets.' The way he broke in the sixth game of the opening set did not conclusively set the tone for what was to follow but it showed that Henman's increasingly versatile strategy of picking the right moment to demonstrate peak aggression, was the right one.

'It was important to stamp my authority on the match,' he said, but admitted a couple of missed chances after he had been 3-1, 30-0 changed the momentum. 'It was pretty nip-and-tuck for the rest of that set. He hits one slightly fortunate return in the tie-break and we're sitting down at one set all. I'd have to say that was pretty depressing.

'All I could do was to be strong mentally and say to myself "well, we started off a best-of-five-set match. Now it's best-of-three and I still fancy my chances." When I was losing my serve in the third set I just thought "OK, it's no big deal, we're back on serve, I'll keep breaking him." That's exactly what I did.'

Nalbandian intimated that he had been seriously inhibited when serving by a strained stomach muscle, a legacy from his long match in the previous round with Karol Kucera. In the end, though, it was Henman's added all-round qualities and his almost impeccable choice of when to serve and volley, and when to stay back and wait for the opportunity to go on the attack, that made more of an impact on the day than either of their serves.

Andre Agassi's dream of becoming the oldest men's singles champion since the advent of Open tennis in 1968 faded when, with his renowned returning ability less effective than usual, he was beaten 6-3, 2-6, 6-7

Tim Henman acknowledges the rapturous reception after he beat David Nalbandian (below) to move into the quarter-finals for a seventh time in eight years.

(4-7), 6-3, 6-4 by Mark Philippoussis. The American, the only former champion still involved, had been Wimbledon champion in 1992, on the third of his 13 visits. He had collected the eighth Grand Slam title of his career at the Australian Open in January and only two weeks before arriving in SW19 had overtaken Lleyton Hewitt to return to the top of the world rankings.

Like Hewitt on Day One, though, he was beaten by a great server. The giant Australian released 46 aces, equalling the record set by Goran Ivanisevic in 1997, although his victory was based on more than just that. 'It's frustrating because we were both looking for chances but he ended up being the one who took them' said Agassi, who promised that, even though he would be 34 by then, he would be back next year. 'Why wouldn't I?' he said. 'I'm a tennis player, this is the place to be and as you get older you are aware of how short-term these opportunities are.'

Only 48 hours after Philippoussis had suggested that Agassi might no longer be the best returner in the game, the 26-year-old was proved correct. Too many of his serves were simply unreturnable and a few more returns than usual missed their target. Agassi had one last major chance, when he held two break points for a 4-2 lead in the final set. 'On one of them [the first] he hit a 120 mph serve,' Agassi recalled. 'I made good contact and it shot back past him. I didn't know if it had hit the baseline — but it hadn't. All I can say is that I made someone play a great match to beat me.'

With hindsight, Roger Federer's 7-6 (7-5), 6-4, 6-4 fourth-round win over the Spaniard, Feliciano Lopez, was one of the most significant moments of the fortnight for, after injuring his back in the warm-up, the fourth seed was periously close to defaulting. He was probably fortunate to face an opponent who lacked the knowledge of how to exploit his lack of mobility on a fast surface.

'I don't know how I won today,' said Federer after receiving intensive treatment on an injury which meant he was not immediately certain that he would be able to play his quarter-final against Sjeng Schalken. 'I'm very lucky to be in the tournament. I was in a lot of pain when it happened and throughout the first set, but at least it got a little better as the match went on and the body warmed up' he added. What Federer did not know at the time was that the Dutchman was also in trouble and was on his way to hospital for a scan on his foot after overcoming Rainer Schuettler 7-5, 6-4, 7-5. Happily both were able to continue otherwise the top half of the draw might have looked even more appealing to Andy Roddick.

While Federer and Schalken were fretting, the resilient American was providing another exhilarating display of torrid serving and bludgeoning forehands as he accounted for Paradorn Srichaphan, 6-4, 3-6, 6-3, 6-2. 'I was trying hard to find a way back but he was just too good, I think he can go on to win it' said Srichaphan, coming to that conclusion because 'he moves well, serves well and hits so well.'

The one dip in Roddick's form — and one that would have alarmed new coach Brad Gilbert, who had yet to see him lose a match — came when the serving rhythm suddenly vanished and even forehand errors crept in from midway through the second set to halfway through the third.

Elsewhere on this day which always offers an embarrassment of riches, with a full round of men's and women's fourth-round matches, Alexander Popp, 14 inches taller than his opponent, outserved Olivier Rochus, Jonas Bjorkman produced more than enough winning serves and backhand passes to account for Max Mirnyi, and Sebastien Grosjean found himself involved

Not even Andre Agassi (above) could withstand the greater all-round power from a jubilant Mark Philippoussis. Similarly, Andy Roddick (right) constantly had Paradorn Srichaphan (below left) at full stretch. Roger Federer (below far right) continued his useful progress against Spain's Feliciano Lopez.

Maria Sharapova's memorable first Wimbledon was brought to an end by fellow Russian Svetlana Kuznetsova, (right centre) but there was no stopping Justine Henin-Hardenne (above right) against Mary Pierce (right) or Jennifer Capriati (far right) against Anastasia Myskina (above centre). Kim Clijsters (top right) also progressed.

Henin-Hardenne • Myskina v Capriati

in another carry-over match when he and Juan Carlos Ferrero were unfinished with Grosjean leading 6-2, 4-6, 7-6 (7-2).

'The Russians are coming' had been a popular cry throughout the first week of the tournament but suddenly all but one them, Svetlana Kuznetsova, who beat another Russian, the charismatic Maria Sharapova, were gone, three of them blown away by the big American guns.

Elena Dementieva lasted only 57 minutes before stalking off without waiting for defending champion, Serena Williams, after another powerful 6-2, 6-2 performance by the top seed. Then Venus Williams clearly took delight at avenging her defeat in the French Open by 18-year-old Vera Zvonareva by trouncing her 6-1, 6-3 in an hour. Venus had taken full advantage following her plaintive cry in Paris that 'I'd love to play her again on a grass court.' Later the sisters were back on court, defending their doubles title with a runaway 6-1, 6-1, second-round victory over the Australians, Alicia Molik and Samantha Stosur.

To complete the Russians' miserable, though hardly unexpected, defeats, Anastasia Myskina not only lost 6-2, 6-3 to Jennifer Capriati in 52 minutes but spent as much time apparently at loggerheads with her coach/boyfriend, Jens Gerlach, trying to find a way of breaking Capriati's forceful command. Kuznetsova's greater experience was eventually decisive, as she fended off a run of eight

games and a service break in the third set, to beat Sharapova, 6-1, 2-6, 7-5 and claim a quarter-final place against Justine Henin-Hardenne, a straightforward 6-3, 6-3 winner against Mary Pierce.

'I can be powerful when I want to be' said the petite Belgian after stretching her winning streak in Grand Slams to 11 matches at the expense of the less mobile Pierce. Reflecting on her winter training in Florida, the nine-stone Belgian said 'I'm much stronger than I was this time last year and that's helping with the mental side of my game as well.'

Kim Clijsters, enjoying the moral support of boyfriend, Lleyton Hewitt, in the player's box for both her singles and doubles matches now that he had time on his hands, moved into the last eight with a 6-3, 6-2 revenge win over her doubles partner, Ai Sugiyama, staying in control throughout after starting by taking the first 13 points. Her next opponent would be Italy's increasingly impressive Silvia Farina Elia, who just outlasted Paola Suarez of Argentina, 7-5, 7-6 (7-3).

Lindsay Davenport completed a line-up for the quarter-finals that included the top six seeds, when she easily cast aside Shinobu Asagoe 6-4, 6-1 and felt herself even better prepared than she had dared to hope after recent injury problems to tackle Venus Williams. 'I have to be aggressive and put pressure on her' Davenport said. 'I'm going to go out there and give it my best shot' — which indeed she did.

Day 8 • Capriati v Williams, S

Serena Williams (right) started to find her best form against Jennifer Capriati in the quarter-finals.

For the first time since 1995, the top four seeds safely reached the semi-finals of the women's singles though there were moments when three of them at least looked vulnerable.

Serena Williams dropped a set and looked decidedly rocky until she at last found the timing off the ground and consistency on serve that had been lacking against Jennifer Capriati. Earlier, both her older sister Venus and Kim Clijsters, who Venus would now meet in the semi-finals, dropped a set as they were given wake-up calls by Lindsay Davenport and the veteran Italian, Silvia Farina Elia, respectively.

Henin-Hardenne looked serenely assured throughout her 6-2, 6-2 defeat of Russian teenager, Svetlana Kuznetsova, the 2001 world junior champion, as she maintained her success without dropping a set. Initially, while still basking in her triumph at Roland Garros and also coming to terms with the hand injury she suffered the weekend before The Championships, she had not looked entirely convincing.

This, though, was the third consecutive match in which she had stepped up the power, the pace and the style — factors that Serena Williams, desperate to take revenge against her for what happened in the semi-finals in Paris, would have duly noted. At 21, Henin-Hardenne was through to her third consecutive semi-final boosted by the experience of already having been a finalist against Venus Williams two years ago. Serena was under no illusions but that, to hold on to the title when she faced Henin-Hardenne two days later, she would have to eradicate the errors that marked her scrappy start against Capriati, the last player to beat her on Centre Court, in the 2001 quarter-finals.

The Capriati challenge against Serena Williams was the most compulsive and also the most competitive, especially when the former kept luring the reigning champion into errors, many of them unforced, in a 27-minute first set. In the end, Serena's more powerful game turned things round for a 2-6, 6-2, 6-3 victory but only after Capriati, undeterred by having lost her seven previous matches against the world champion, matched her serve for serve, forehand drive for ever more acutely angled forehand drive in some titanic rallies, one spanning 32 strokes at the heart of the battle.

Capriati had not had to do much more than keep the ball in play during the first set. Williams was broken twice and was a shade fortunate not to fall behind in the fifth game of the second set. Yet somehow the ace she produced to save a break point she had offered

her opponent with a wild overhead acted like a beacon of inspiration, or perhaps as personal rebuke for thereafter Capriati's hold on the match was quickly loosened.

It was not so much that her game wavered; her determination and fighting spirit never faltered even though her fierce driving from the baseline did become increasingly predictable in a match that for most of the time would have been more suited to a clay court than grass. The transformation really came about because Williams began cutting out the errors and Capriati was able to claim 'I don't think I gave her the match, she really had to elevate her game. On the day I don't think anyone else could have beaten me. She served a couple at 119 mph. That's why she's number one.'

Venus Williams was already a break up against Davenport before the rain that had been forecast to threaten the tennis for most of the day drove them off court for 1 hour 21 minutes and, although she immediately double-faulted when they resumed and then lost her serve, it was only in the second set that she was almost driven off course by the 1999 champion. 'This is the round when all of us have to lift our game,' Davenport had said before going on court and she responded perfectly. A forehand that had strayed badly for a while in the middle of the opening set became a major force, frequently biting deep into the corners.

The sixth game of the set looked as if it might even turn the whole match. Davenport, leading 3-2, saved three break points, two of them with scorching forehand cross-court winners, the other with an ace and she went on to level the match with a flourish. Yet her revival faded just as abruptly. She was always under pressure after double-faulting on the first point at 1-2 in the final set and Williams, having broken with an unreturnable backhand, raced on to take the last 11 points of the match.

Venus was all smiles and no wonder. The despair she felt after her fourth-round defeat in Paris by the young Russian, Vera Zvonareva, whom she had soundly spanked here on Monday, was, like the abdominal muscle strain she was suffering from at the time, hopefully behind her. She could hardly

Richard Williams (above), father of the sisters who between them have held the Wimbledon trophy for four years, must have been pleased by the way Venus held firm despite one marvellous set from Lindsay Davenport (below), watched by celebrity guests, cricketer Graham Gooch, Sir Cliff Richard and Cilla Black.

have imagined then that another injury was on the horizon.

Clijsters, the only semi-finalist yet to win a Grand Slam crown, sprayed errors all round the court, especially off the forehand in the first set against 31-year-old Elia, making her first quarter-final appearance at this level in 41 Grand Slam tournaments but then Clijsters took 12 of the remaining 13 games to win 5-7, 6-0, 6-1. 'It was a matter of finding my footwork and serving better' said the Belgian, who is no stranger to such spectacular, though usually temporary, lapses.

It was also a matter of overcoming the bee sting she suffered when she walked out to receive serve in the tenth game of the first set. She simply pulled her shirt down over the wound and carried on in such a nonchalant manner that it was only afterwards when she mentioned it, and said how happy she was not to have let it distract her for more than a few minutes, that anyone really knew what had happened. 'I was just pleased I didn't blow up' said Clijsters, meaning it in an allergic sense. Instead it was Elia who suffered a reaction, seemingly so stunned to have won the first set that she had nothing left to withstand the Clijsters onslaught that followed.

Meanwhile Sebastien Grosjean spent 67 minutes winning a fourth-set tie-break 7-3 against Juan Carlos Ferrero in their match which had been unfinished overnight to become the French lamb Henman would be hoping to slaughter the next day in the quarter-finals. As is so often the case in Grosjean's matches, he remained calm under pressure and waited for the right moment to strike. Ferrero threatened early on to shock him by going to the net but Grosjean patiently picked off the Spaniard with elegant backhands and whipped forehands as he awaited his chance.

Todd Woodbridge and Jonas Bjorkman moved to within two matches of retaining the men's doubles title after outclassing the seventh-seeded Australian pair, Wayne Arthurs and Paul Hanley, 6-3, 6-4, 7-5 and there was further encouragement for them when Mark Knowles and Daniel Nestor, the team they beat in the 2002 final, were surprisingly upset by Israeli qualifiers, Jonathan Erlich and Andy Ram.

Despite holding the title, Woodbridge,

Kim Clijsters (left) was all smiles against Silvia Farina Elia (above), but only after she recovered from losing the first set. Meanwhile, Justine Henin-Hardenne (right) gave nothing away against Svetlana Kuznetsova (below).

Juan Carlos Ferrero was in fine form in his unfinished match against Sebastien Grosjean (above), although he ultimately lost and there were moments when he could not believe he had misfired and sought reassurance from a line umpire.

Right: Time for the Williams sisters to talk tactics as their hopes of winning the ladies' doubles title evaporated.

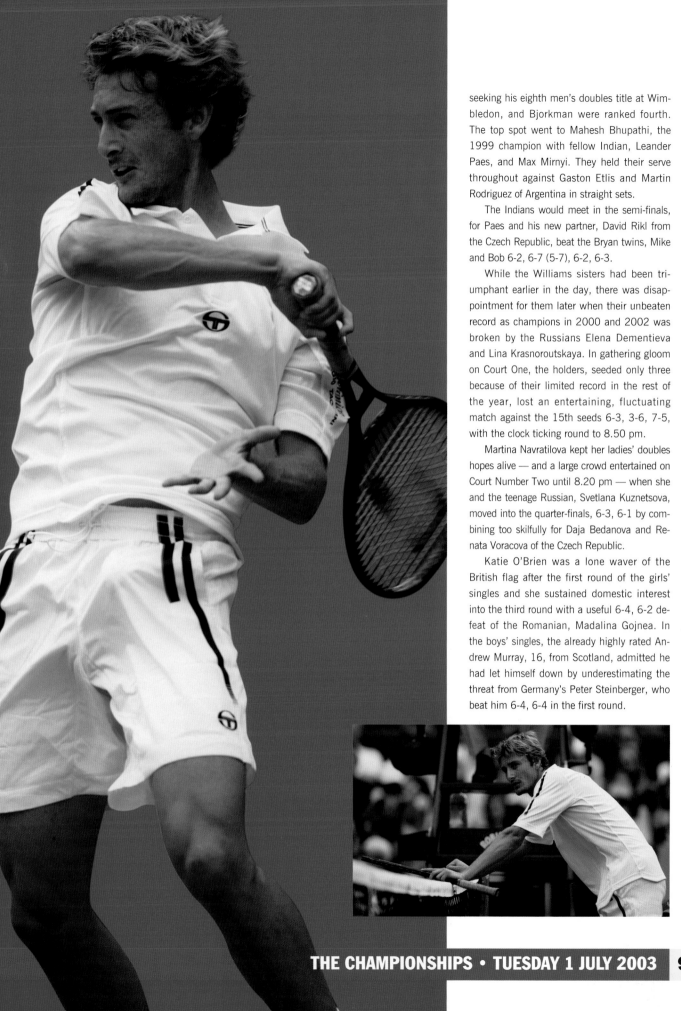

seeking his eighth men's doubles title at Wimbledon, and Bjorkman were ranked fourth. The top spot went to Mahesh Bhupathi, the 1999 champion with fellow Indian, Leander Paes, and Max Mirnyi. They held their serve throughout against Gaston Etlis and Martin Rodriguez of Argentina in straight sets.

The Indians would meet in the semi-finals, for Paes and his new partner, David Rikl from the Czech Republic, beat the Bryan twins, Mike and Bob 6-2, 6-7 (5-7), 6-2, 6-3.

While the Williams sisters had been triumphant earlier in the day, there was disappointment for them later when their unbeaten record as champions in 2000 and 2002 was broken by the Russians Elena Dementieva and Lina Krasnoroutskaya. In gathering gloom on Court One, the holders, seeded only three because of their limited record in the rest of the year, lost an entertaining, fluctuating match against the 15th seeds 6-3, 3-6, 7-5, with the clock ticking round to 8.50 pm.

Martina Navratilova kept her ladies' doubles hopes alive — and a large crowd entertained on Court Number Two until 8.20 pm — when she and the teenage Russian, Svetlana Kuznetsova, moved into the quarter-finals, 6-3, 6-1 by combining too skilfully for Daja Bedanova and Renata Voracova of the Czech Republic.

Katie O'Brien was a lone waver of the British flag after the first round of the girls' singles and she sustained domestic interest into the third round with a useful 6-4, 6-2 defeat of the Romanian, Madalina Gojnea. In the boys' singles, the already highly rated Andrew Murray, 16, from Scotland, admitted he had let himself down by underestimating the threat from Germany's Peter Steinberger, who beat him 6-4, 6-4 in the first round.

THE CHAMPIONSHIPS WIMBLEDON

WEDNESDAY 2 JULY

Day 9

It had probably been asking too much for The Championships to escape the worst of what the weathermen had been indicating for a third day in succession. And so it was.

For although Tim Henman and Sebastien Grosjean were able to walk out on Centre Court on time for the first of the men's singles quarter-finals they had only been in action for 15 minutes when they were off again. It was the first of four interruptions on this day of increasing frustration for players — not least those who waited in vain all day to play — spectators and officials.

When play was finally abandoned for the day at 7.21 pm on Centre Court and a few minutes later on Number One Court, not one of the day's four principal contests had been resolved, including the showpiece contest between Britain's Tim Henman, seeking his fifth semi-final place in six years and the Frenchman, Sebastien Grosjean, through to the last eight at The Championships for the first time.

Since Henman first made a major impact on the lawns of The All England Club in 1996 by saving match points to beat Yevgeny Kafelnikov in the first round, barely two weeks after the Russian had won the French Open, every match he has played at Wimbledon has gripped the public. And after the way the draw had seemingly opened up for him this time with former champion, Andre Agassi, out of the way and no other seed after Grosjean barring his route to the final, 'Henmania' among his fans and the media was rife once again.

During 2 hours 28 minutes of tennis that was as uncertain as the weather, Henman followers were in turn bewildered, elated, and ultimately left fretting overnight when play was abandoned for the day with Grosjean, having saved four set points in the opening set, leading 7-6 (10-8), 3-6, 6-3, 1-2, with his serve to come.

Although the light drizzle that had started falling two games earlier had stopped, Grosjean twice complained to umpire Carlos Ramos that the surface was too slippery and dangerous for them to continue. Referee Alan Mills, summoned at the end of the third game, agreed and the television microphones picked up him telling the umpire 'There's rain

in the air, it's too slippery, there's fading light, that's it for the night.'

If it had been an on-off-on-off day from the weather point of view, down-up-down-up and then down again was the best way to sum up the progress of Henman's prospects. He had been looking to start as smartly as against David Nalbandian but it was Grosjean who sprinted out of the blocks in awesome fashion.

By the time they went off for the first of the rain breaks, Grosjean was leading 4-1, having powered two passes off the forehand and two more struck with great precision off the backhand to break in the fourth game. His tally of outright winners had already reached seven, in addition to four aces.

The delay gave Henman an opportunity to draw breath and ponder. It was not so much that he had started badly; simply that the wily, pugnacious and versatile Grosjean had not put a foot or a shot wrong. Even so, there was no immediate relief for the crowd's favourite son.

When they returned after a break of 62 minutes, Henman double-faulted to give Grosjean the chance for a double break that he accepted by forcing his opponent to volley over the baseline. Yet they had only been back on court for four minutes before the covers were needed again and this time it was clearly a reprieve. The rest of the set, after an interruption of 38 minutes, was great theatre.

Grosjean, serving for the set, suddenly seemed mysteriously sluggish. Henman sensed the change, attacked vigorously and not only broke back to 2-5 with a chip and charge and an inspired backhand volley but then forced another error from the Frenchman. Two games later, encouraged this time by a floating backhand that dropped meticulously into the corner, Henman reached 30-40 on his opponent's serve and a stunned Grosjean netted a forehand to lose his second break as well.

The crowd were on their feet for the start of a thrilling tie-break, during which there was an early exchange of mini-breaks before Henman, serving at 3-4, took a leaf out of Grosjean's book with a classic backhand cross-court winner, followed it up with another successful chip and charge and, lo and behold, went on to hold three set points. They all, though, escaped him.

Henman saved the first break point against him at 6-7 with a masterly serve. Yet after moving to his own fourth set point with a wonderfully brave second delivery deep into the corner, he lost this as well by netting a backhand. Two points later, Grosjean pocketed the set with another of those enviable cross-court returns.

Henman v Grosjean • Day 9

The covers were needed most of the day but the bouts of rain failed to dent the enthusiasm of the fans.

Day 9 · Philippoussis v Popp

Alexander Popp, playing in his second Wimbledon quarter-final, won the first two sets against Mark Philippoussis.

scintillating service returns to break for 5-3 before serving out for the set.

Naturally enough play on Court One was disrupted just as often and we discovered afterwards that Philippoussis had advice and counselling during the rain breaks, not just from his father, Nick, who had taken over from Peter McNamara as his coach a few months earlier but also from the current Australian Davis Cup captain, John Fitzgerald, and his predecessor, Neale Fraser.

He needed it. After two sets, Philippoussis was trailing 4-6, 4-6, constantly being punished by the blistering returns from the 6ft 7in Popp, whenever the German was offered an inviting second serve or a mid-court ball in the middle of a rally.

The turning point began at 3-2 in the third when Philippoussis, who had turned his back on the distracting party scene in Miami for a quieter life in the even sunnier San Diego, earned a break point for the first time since the opening set, grabbed it and went on to take the set 6-3.

It prompted an altogether new sense of purpose in him that he maintained beyond another delay so that, by the time they were left kicking their heels overnight, he had levelled the score in sets and was serving first at 2-2 in the fifth.

A handful of doubles and a clutch of junior matches also managed to take place. The most significant included progress by two of the top four seeded teams in the ladies' doubles although the match that attracted the most attention was also stopped by the weather. Kim Clijsters and Ai Sugiyama were leading Svetlana Kuznetsova and the redoubtable Martina Navratilova.

In the juniors the British outlook was as bleak as the weather. Joshua Goodall, the only one among 11 boys in the draw to make it beyond the second round, was outclassed by the Czech Republic's top-seeded Tomas Berdych, 6-2, 6-3 while Katie O'Brien, the only British female to win a match in either the ladies' or girls' singles, went down in the third round to Finland's 11th-seeded Emma Laine, 6-1, 7-5. It was Britain's weakest showing in the junior singles for ten years — and the rain just added to the feeling of despondency.

There were times mid-way through the second set when Henman's first serve percentage dropped so alarmingly that one wondered if his shoulder was causing fresh discomfort. Yet, having rescued the loss of his serve in the opening game, his level soared again, especially when he broke for 5-3, albeit with the help of a lucky net cord on a service return and he deservedly served out to level the match.

At 1-1 in the third, back came the rain, this time heavier than ever and it was 2 hours 7 minutes before they re-appeared under still-threatening skies. As in the first set, Grosjean snapped straight back into top gear, with four

Mark Philippoussis had to dig deep to stay in the match, encouraged by his vocal fans.

Below: Katie O'Brien, the last British survivor in the girls' singles.

Bottom right: Ai Sugiyama and Kim Clijsters plot doubles tactics.

A dramatic example of Venus Williams's athleticism.

Not for the first time, it was agony without the ecstacy for Britain's Tim Henman, as his tenth bid to attain the one title he had dreamed of winning since he was little more than a toddler fell short. And not for the first time, either, the men upstaged the women who would normally have had the scene to themselves for their semi-finals.

The feeling of despair and emptiness engulfing Henman, as he sliced a backhand service return into the net so that Sebastien Grosjean would take the place he had so much wanted to fill in the semi-finals, was gruesomely evident.

Although he managed one brief wave to a crowd that had lived every point with him during the 32 minutes it took the Frenchman to complete his 7-6 (10-8), 3-6, 6-3, 6-4 victory, after it had been suspended by the weather overnight, his dejection was complete.

He could barely lift his head to appreciate the warmth of the support or the sympathy for him all round Centre Court, even though in the final analysis, as he admitted, he had lost because he had not been quite good enough.

'Over the whole course of the match his standard of play was better than mine,' Henman admitted. 'If I break it down, he served better than me. For a guy that's 5ft 9in to serve as well as he did and consistently well, was a huge aspect. I didn't volley well either so, in most aspects, I didn't match up well and that's disappointing.'

He conceded that 'nothing really hides my disappointment and frustration at the outcome' of his quarter-final. And when asked if his best chance of winning Wimbledon had come and gone, he replied: 'Maybe. Perhaps my chances are getting less but it won't stop me coming back and trying. You've got to believe. If you don't believe in yourself, you've got no shot.'

Henman has been so teasingly close so often to becoming the first British player to reach the men's singles final since Bunny Austin in 1938 and, amid the inevitable disappointment, his achievements in reaching the semi-finals four times — and only failing to reach the last eight once in a span of eight years — should not be forgotten and undervalued.

Not that such statistics eased his pain. 'I

don't feel any sense of achievement' he said. 'I heard the other day that Jimmy [Connors] and Pete [Sampras] were the only other guys to have made the second week here for eight years in a row so perhaps I should feel some sense of achievement. But I don't right now. With my own expectations and the way the fortnight unfolded, I'm massively disappointed.'

Overnight Henman had trailed by two sets to one, after missing four set points in the opening set to an opponent who had done a fine job in masking his recurring groin strain that, he said, made it difficult for him to push off on the forehand side. Grosjean admitted that the rain the previous night had helped him considerably. 'He was playing better at the time and I wasn't moving that well,' he conceded.

Even with a 2-1 lead when they resumed, the odds were against Henman but it was a new day, a time for fresh hope, even if it hardly seemed like that when further rain again delayed the proceedings. Although Henman held his first service game of the day for 3-2, it was only after Grosjean had demonstrated that his backhand winners were as lethal as ever. Two games later they were responsible for creating the one service break that Grosjean needed to open the door for him to reach the semi-finals.

With Henman serving at 3-3, 15-15, a quick flick of the wrist was all that seemed necessary for the skilful Grosjean to deliver a dipping return that his opponent was unable to scoop back off his feet. Next came a crunching return that set up the chance for Grosjean to put an easy forehand into space and earn two break points. One was sufficient. He took it in spectacular fashion — an almost round-arm backhand from virtually behind him after Henman must have thought that his brilliant half-volley pick-up from nearly on the ground would have been sufficient.

More breathtaking backhands brought up a first match point but for once the Grosjean rasping forehand lacked both height and direction. After a growl — or perhaps something stronger — under his breath when a ringing mobile telephone distracted him while serving on his first game point, Henman held to 4-5 but there was the feeling of inevitability when he walked out to receive in the tenth

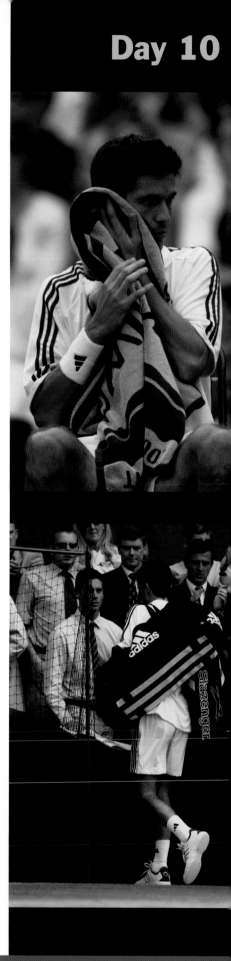

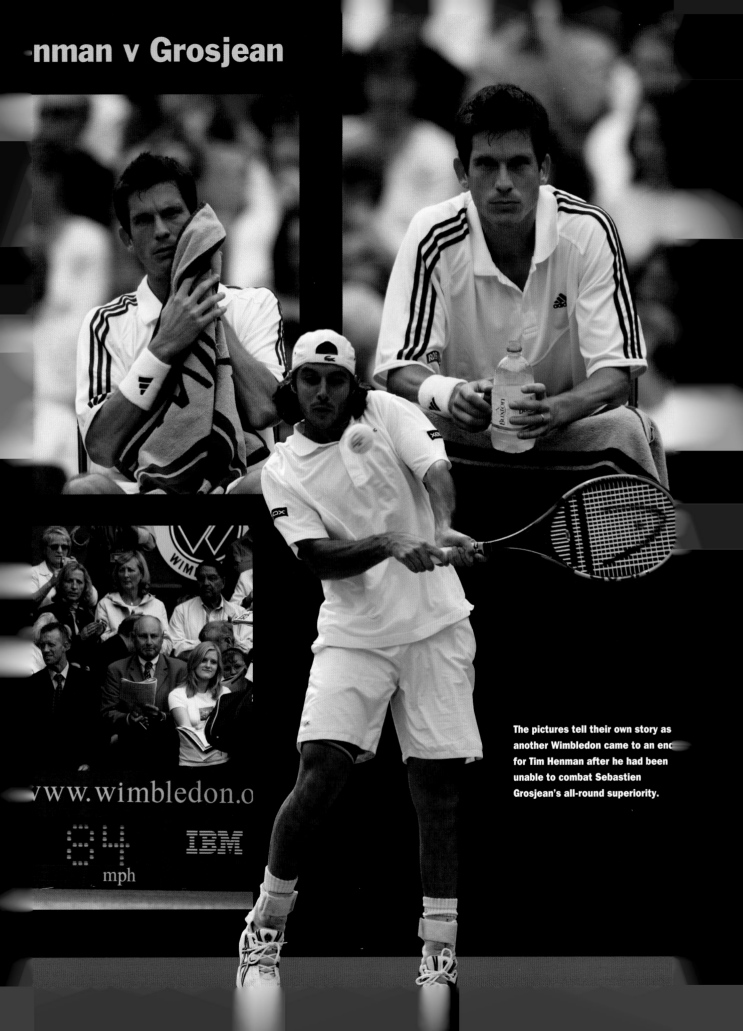

nman v Grosjean

www.wimbledon.o

84 mph

IBM

The pictures tell their own story as another Wimbledon came to an end for Tim Henman after he had been unable to combat Sebastien Grosjean's all-round superiority.

game. An overhit backhand, an ace and a failed service return swept Grosjean into the last four for the first time — and a meeting with Mark Philippoussis.

Just three weeks after wondering if his grass-court season would be as unrewarding as most of his tennis in the first half of the year, the tall, powerful Australian also became a first-time Wimbledon semi-finalist when he struck another 34 aces against Germany's Alexander Popp, taking his total for the tournament to 153. They contributed greatly to him completing the recovery he had started the night before, 4-6, 4-6, 6-3, 6-3, 8-6.

It was just as well his serve was once again highlighting his nickname, 'The Scud', for Popp, though seemingly facing an uphill struggle after losing his two-sets lead overnight, continued to return spectacularly from the resumption at 2-2 in the final set.

Asked what reaching the penultimate stage at The Championships meant to him after being out of the final stage spotlight at a Grand Slam since losing to fellow country-man, Pat Rafter, in the 1998 US Open final, he smiled and said 'God, it's been so long.'

It was perhaps only fitting that his game should so suddenly take shape again at a tournament where things had started to go so seriously wrong. Playing Sampras in the 1999 quarter-finals, he took the first set in devastating fashion but then suffered the major cartilage injury that had since needed three operations, confined him to a wheel-chair for two months and been told that he would never play top-level tennis again.

The only break during Part Two of the match against Popp, that had been littered with missed break points by both men, came in the final game when Philippoussis stepped up the pressure, starting with a forehand service return winner. He reached match point with a stunning forehand pass down the line, hit as he slipped and slithered to the ground. He took it by pouncing on a nervous second serve and his opponent then placed a weak backhand into the net.

Popp, who has a British passport because his mother comes from Wolverhampton, stood dejectedly, hands on hips, contemplating what might have been had he taken any

of the four break points offered him in the last two Philippoussis service games, especially one at 6-6. 'I thought I hit a good return and follow-up passing shot but he made an incredible dive to play a brilliant cross-court volley,' he said sadly. 'I mean, I didn't do anything wrong on that point. He came up with a shot that he could maybe only play once in ten times.'

That point was symptomatic of a high-quality final set that really could have gone either way.

The other half of the draw provided the expected semi-finalists, Andy Roddick versus Roger Federer, in a much more straightforward manner. Sjeng Schalken's badly bruised foot proved far more of a problem than Federer's dodgy back, although the Dutchman was sporting enough to admit that even if fully fit, he would have struggled to combat his opponent's impressive serve-and-volley game. Federer eased to a 6-3, 6-4, 6-4 victory in 98 minutes in a match which lacked some of its expected lustre by having to be switched from Centre Court to Number Two Court to overcome the backlog caused by Wednesday's weather.

Schalken needed an injection before the match in an attempt to reduce the inflammation but he started feeling the pain again after only three games although he soldiered on for almost an hour, by which time he was on the verge of going two sets down, before calling for a trainer. It clearly helped because, with Federer starting to make errors, Schalken moved to a 4-1 lead in the third set before his Swiss opponent reacted positively to a potential crisis and took five consecutive games for victory.

Roddick's 6-4, 6-2, 6-4 was as thorough and effective as the score indicated. He hustled Bjorkman, 11 years his senior, out of Number One Court in 92 minutes. His ferocious serve delivered 14 aces and many times that number of other service winners. The pattern of the match was similar throughout — Roddick surging through his service games without much difficulty and Bjorkman working feverishly to hold his, often after several deuces.

The end of the road in singles for Jonas Bjorkman (top) and Sjeng Schalken (above) against Andy Roddick (right) and Roger Federer (far right) respectively.

Roddick

Day 10 • Williams, V v Clijsters

Kim Clijsters started purposefully enough against Venus Williams (right) but was unable to sustain her form after her opponent needed treatment for injury and then benefited from a rain break.

On paper the semi-finals of the ladies' singles promised a full panoply of emotions as well as two matches likely to be fiercely contested. That was certainly so in the case of Venus Williams fending off severe pain from an abdominal injury and then a hip problem to beat Kim Clijsters, 4-6, 6-3, 6-1. The drama began to unfold in the second game. Clijsters, who had already broken in the previous game, tempted Williams into the net with the obvious intention of trying to pass her yet again. As the former champion galloped forward, however, smacking a double-handed backhand into the net, there was an ominous squeal and she could be seen wincing as she grabbed her stomach.

At the end of the game she went off for a medical time-out and was gone for almost ten minutes. 'I just couldn't calm myself down, all I could think of was the injury, I was in real trouble,' Williams admitted

When they resumed, Clijsters naturally did everything she could to exploit the American's injury, pulling her first one way and then the other, as well as tormenting her even more with lobs that evoked more painful winces. Then at the end of the set the rain came and as Venus said 'I think that saved me. Serena came into the locker room and told me to calm down and my mother added "If you're going to play, play. If not, don't." So I gritted my teeth and started fighting.'

She broke Clijsters three times in taking the second set and turned the match decisively her way in the third game of the final set. Moments after Clijsters had celebrated a

majestic lob, Williams wore her into submission in a marathon rally and never looked back, losing only one game in the set.

If anyone had questioned the mental pain Serena Williams had endured when losing to Justine Henin-Hardenne in Paris four weeks earlier, the evidence was striking in the powerfully ruthless and unforgiving way in which she exacted revenge, 6-3, 6-2. She raced to a 4-0 lead by regularly pounding full-length groundstrokes and although Henin-Hardenne broke back to 3-4, the wasteful game in which the Belgian was then broken was virtually an admission that this would be another Williams day. The exaggerated roar of delight from Williams when she lambasted an overhead on the first point as she served for the set, was characteristic of her unyielding approach. The lightweight Henin-Hardenne had no answer to the pace, weight and accuracy of the shots raining down on her. The champion, it seemed, had been keeping her best for when it was most needed.

Action in the men's doubles was restricted to just five points and two minutes — not because of the rain delays earlier but because of a gentleman's agreement between the four semi-final pairings to help those still in the mixed doubles, to make up for lost time. Originally Max Mirnyi and Mahesh Bhupathi, the top seeds, would have expected to play again after putting the finishing touches to their 7-6 (7-2), 7-6 (7-3), 6-3, defeat of the Czechs, Martin Damm and Cyril Suk but it was postponed for 24 hours.

The decision helped not only Todd Woodbridge, partnered by Svetlana Kuznetsova to wrap up a 6-3, 6-1 second-round win but Leander Paes to help make sure that Martina Navratilova's dream of a record 20th Wimbledon title stayed alive by beating Peter Luczak and Christina Wheeler 6-4, 6-2 in the third round of the mixed.

Among the juniors, Katie O'Brien, the most successful British player in the singles by reaching the third round, was unable to follow that up in the girls' doubles when she and Georgie Stoop struggled from the outset against Finland's Emma Laine, the girl who had knocked her out of the singles, and Nadja Pavic of Croatia. The score was 6-1, 6-2.

Henin-Hardenne

Justine Henin-Hardenne was overpowered by the fiercely competitive Serena Williams (inset).

COURT

4

THE CHAMPIONSHIPS
WIMBLEDON

FRIDAY 4 JULY

Day 11

Federer v Roddick · Day 11

For the first time since 1982 both semi-finals in the men's singles were decided in straight sets. Not that anyone was complaining for, after a master-class of serving from Mark Philippoussis in beating Sebastien Grosjean, Roger Federer provided a memorable all-court display to savour against the bookmakers' favourite for the title, Andy Roddick.

'People who come here understand their tennis so that's what makes it so special' said the 21-year-old Swiss as he reflected on how the crowd had been on their feet at his moment of 7-6 (8-6), 6-3, 6-3 triumph in 1 hour 43 minutes.

This was no ordinary response. It lasted the full three minutes that it took for the players to congratulate each other, gather their chattels and depart a Centre Court glowing not just from the sunshine but the impact of his most gloriously authoritative and artistic tennis. It was about as faultless as one can hope to see on grass — the most consistently supreme tennis on Centre Court since Pete Sampras's imperious form in the 1999 final against Andre Agassi.

'He plays like they used to play' enthused Boris Becker in his commentary for BBC Television. Federer would have appreciated that, for long before he first arrived at Wimbledon and fell in love with the place — and more particularly playing on grass — as a junior, the fearless German and the elegantly accomplished Stefan Edberg were his heroes.

There was a hint of both of them in the way he played, plus a hint of Manuel Santana's feathered touch as he set about ruthlessly demolishing a Roddick game that had already brought the American the Stella Artois title and an unbeaten record from ten matches on grass in this English summer.

Federer's tactics were evident and, so far as Roddick was concerned, irresistible. The venom was removed from the young American's serve by Federer's subtle mix of blocking some first returns and then scheming his way into position to put away a winner or immediately unleashing a rasping return that was either a clean winner or rocked Roddick so much back on his heels that he was vulnerable to whatever followed.

Roddick had already had a taste of Federer's ability to cope with a serve that so readily threatens others and went into the match with a 0-3 record from their previous contests, but managed only four aces. Federer, with a service action that was as smooth as silk but as damaging as a bazooka, struck 17. Even when Roddick did make the return, it was, more often than not, only a temporary reprieve because Federer, also blanketing the

Roger Federer's serve was in full working order as he outclassed Andy Roddick (below).

net and volleying more effectively than even his most admiring supporters could remember, allowed him only 14 points off his 15 service games.

The other staggering statistic that needs to be remembered was that Federer hit 61 winners and made only 12 unforced errors. It was no wonder that more than once Roddick could do nothing but break into a broad grin after being left helpless against a barrage of winners, the most fantastic of which was probably the crunching forehand that completed the second set — the 17th stroke of a rip-roaring, fierce driving rally.

Roddick had been offered just one chance. After trailing 2-4 in the tie-break, he clawed his way back and, at 5-5, whacked a huge forehand that caught Federer off-guard and provided him with a set point on his own serve. Yet with Federer's court seemingly at his mercy as he came in behind his serve, Roddick impetuously snatched a forehand into the net. Federer added insult to injury by impeccably demonstrating how a forehand should be struck, albeit off the ground this time, and then hit another winning serve to establish an initiative he never looked like sacrificing while winning 7-6 (8-6), 6-3, 6-3.

In the other semi-final the first-set tie-break was also crucial. The opening games had been dominated by the particular skills of both players, Philippoussis with his serve, Grosjean with that deceptive mixture of placement and spin. Indeed going into his sixth service game at 5-6, the Frenchman had yielded only one point on serve. Suddenly, though, he was at 15-40, facing the formidable sight of the 6ft 4in, sturdily built Australian bearing down on him as he increasingly came in behind service returns. A delicate drop volley and a searing forehand and then another awesome drop shot carried 5ft 9in Grosjean back to dry land — though it was not long before he lost his footing again and slipped back into dangerous waters.

At 2-2 in the tie-break, Philippoussis double-faulted. It was Grosjean's chance to strike but having darted forward well enough, the 13th seed not only dumped what should have been a forehand drop shot into the net but then wafted a backhand cross-court beyond the sideline. Philippoussis demonstrated his

Sebastien Grosjean (above) ran out of ideas and steam against the power of Mark Philippoussis (far right) as did Andy Roddick (right) when he suffered the same fate against Roger Federer.

While Mark Philippoussis was beating Sebastien Grosjean to reach the men's singles final, television cameras picked up how the Australian had written 'andras' on the plaster protecting his thumb and 'pothia' on another covering his forefinger of his left hand. Greek scholars said that translated they meant 'man' and 'desire', two words that aptly described this athlete with Greek ancestry, who already had a tattoo of Alexander the Great on his shoulder.

gratitude for such a let-off with two more pummelled second serves and then a clever backhand service return that clinched the set.

It continued to go pear-shaped for the Frenchman, who looked increasingly weary, when he was immediately broken in the opening game of the second set. In the space of seven minutes the whole pattern of the match had been transformed.

Thereafter Philippoussis maintained a firm grip and, although Grosjean managed a couple more cherished examples of his ability to lure opponents forward and then torment them by caressing the most perfectly judged lobs, that alone was never going to be enough. His best Wimbledon had run into the buffers in the shape of an Australian starting at last, he hoped, to live a dream.

Not all the excitement, gilded with sentiment, was confined to the men's singles. In the three main doubles events, important happenings were also unfolding. Although Martina Navratilova and Svetlana Kuznetsova were unable to build on their success in the opening set when their match against the second seeds, Kim Clijsters and Ai Sugiyama, resumed, losing 4-6, 6-2, 6-4, Navratilova continued to set the pace in the mixed doubles. She and Leander Paes won a thrilling quarter-final contest when they upset the seedings by beating the young American doubles specialists, Mike Bryan and Lisa Raymond, 5-7, 7-6 (7-3), 6-4.

In an exciting, sometimes light-hearted contest, with which BBC2 stayed until the end at 8.35 pm, the 46-year-old and her Indian partner had been perilously close to a straight-sets defeat. Navratilova took a painful blow when an acrobatic intervention by Bryan at the net struck her on the buttock but she continued to demonstrate her own agility and quick thinking at the net in a manner which prompted Paes more than once to bow in mock worship of her venerable talent. Clijsters and Sugiyama meanwhile went on from ending Navratilova's chances in the ladies' doubles by reaching the final with an entertaining 6-1, 0-6, 6-4 victory over Raymond and Lindsay Davenport. Waiting for them in the final were top seeds Virginia Ruano Pascual and Paola Suarez, who recovered from

losing the first set to beat Elena Dementieva and Lina Krasnoroutskaya, 3-6, 6-1, 6-2.

Todd Woodbridge was also still chasing what might have been called double doubles honours: the mixed title as well as a staggering eighth men's triumph. He and Jonas Bjorkman arrived at Court Three without dropping a set and although the Israeli qualifiers, Jonathan Erlich and Andy Ram, ruined that record, the fourth seeds lifted their form after the setback and won 6-2, 4-6, 6-2, 6-1 in a minute over two hours. Their opponents in the final would be Max Mirnyi and Mahesh Bhupathi, the top seeds, who took 2 hours 46 minutes to beat David Rikl from the Czech Republic and Leander Paes, with whom Bhupathi won the title in 1999, 6-7 (6-8), 6-4, 7-6 (9-7), 6-3.

One crumb of British comfort remained in the junior events. Andrew Murray and Tom Rushby, though unseeded, overwhelmed Sweden's Pablo Figueroa and Mexican, Luis Flores, 6-2, 6-3 to reach the doubles semi-finals for the loss of only ten games in four sets.

Doubles retains a magic of its own at Wimbledon, especially when demonstrated by four of the finest pairs in the world.

Clockwise from top left: Todd Woodbridge and Jonas Bjorkman, Martina Navratilova and Svetlana Kuznetsova, Paola Suarez and Virginia Ruano Pascual, Ai Sugiyama and Kim Clijsters.

David Rikl, at full stretch, reaching for a backhand as he and Leander Paes tackled Mahesh Bhupathi and Max Mirnyi, seen racing across the back of the court.

SATURDAY 5 JULY

Day 12

Serena Williams predictably strengthened her hold on the world number one ranking and took the first prize worth £535,000 as the trophy remained in the grip of the Williams family for a fourth consecutive year. It was Serena's sixth consecutive victory over her older sister, the 2000–2001 champion, a fact that hardly supported the widely held theory that their father, Richard, believed they should share and share alike.

Every Wimbledon final is a special occasion though this one, for a variety of reasons, not least the impact of the stomach and hip injuries Venus took with her into the final, was not one to linger in the memory. The first set was fascinating, if only because Serena seemed either unwilling or unable to capitalise upon her sister's physical limitations and found herself trailing 0-3 as a consequence in next to no time.

True, there were moments in all three sets when Venus forgot about the pain and Serena forgot that it was her sister on the other side of the net so that they then engaged in boisterous, fulsome rallies. Yet they were disappointingly few, and one could never lose the impression that the crowd, reluctant as ever in such circumstances to support one sibling at the expense of the other, had been expecting and hoping for more.

The frustrating dilemma for those striving to boost the image of women's tennis is that while the Williams sisters are clearly two of their finest players and most marketable assets, they only truly impress on court when playing genuine rivals — not another member of the family.

It was not just that there were so few hard-hitting rallies or robustly competitive points to reveal their respective, considerable talents between passages of wasteful, erratic play as

No lack of effort from Serena Williams (opposite) as she eventually took control in the ladies' singles final against her injured sister, Venus.

Day 12 • Williams, S v Williams, V

Venus Williams was in such pain from her
strained stomach muscles that referee Alan
Mills called for the trainer.

Far right: Painted faces in the crowd
brightened an otherwise overcast final
Saturday but Serena (below left) and Venus
both managed a smile in offering mutual
congratulations and commiserations.

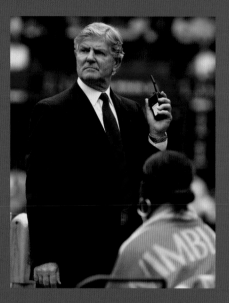

Serena increased her career advantage over Venus to 7-5. The score was 4-6, 6-4, 6-2.

The biggest problem, that is almost always there when they play each other, was that there was no real depth in the passion one would normally expect from players in a Grand Slam singles final. It is difficult to see how that situation can change. It was most obviously missing at the moment of victory when Serena's reaction was depressingly subdued.

To what extent Serena felt it was a hollow victory because of Venus's injury, or whether either of them will ever properly cherish winning a major title at the expense of the other, we will never know. For the most part — though Serena's outburst against Justine Henin-Hardenne and the barracking French crowd a month earlier was an exception — they keep their inner feelings secret.

Venus admitted that had it not been the Wimbledon final she probably would have withdrawn rather than risk further injury from the hip problem she sustained when she did the splits in front of the Royal Box in the semi-final against Kim Clijsters, at the time already worried about strained stomach muscles.

'I came out because I thought the fans deserved a final' she told a crowd that clearly appreciated her gesture otherwise they would have had to settle for the first walkover in a final since the American Frank Shields gave Sidney Wood a free passage in the 1931 men's singles climax, rather than aggravate an injury two weeks before the Davis Cup final. How things have changed?

Aware of the outcry when she withdrew from a semi-final against Serena barely 30 minutes before they were due to play in Indian Wells three years earlier, the older sister said, 'It's just hard these days. Serena and I have taken a lot of flak, so I felt I had to take one for the team.'

Richard Williams, their father who flew home after the semi-finals saying 'My job is done, now it's up to them,' must take some of the blame for the conspiracy theories that all too often abound when they play. He and the girls will, it seems, forever have to live with the aftermath of him allowing the impression to gain credence before their first Wimbledon clash in 2000 that he would decide which of

his daughters would win. He has since denied such allegations vehemently but the damage was done.

Serena insisted that the reason Venus surged into a 3-0 lead dropping only two points, and held four points for 4-0, was because she 'maybe started out a bit slow' and 'was making a few too many errors'. 'But at the same time' she added 'she was just running me back and forth and blasting winners when she saw an opportunity.'

Fair enough, except that Serena's average first serves were closer to 100 mph than the 120 mph she often achieves and almost inevitably that led to a presumption even on the part of BBC TV commentators. John McEnroe and Tracy Austin, both former Grand Slam winners, felt that perhaps because she knew her sister was being restricted by injury she was holding something back.

Not so, Serena assured us later though when two sisters have been brought up almost as one, quite apart from living, practising and often socialising with each other, that could easily be true without them even being aware. Asked how difficult it was to keep her focus when Venus had to leave the court for treatment, in obvious distress and with a possibility she might not be able to continue in the third set, Serena said: 'I can't say it was that difficult. I just kept thinking "this is Wimbledon" And who knows when I'll have this opportunity again. That's what kept me motivated.'

Much has been made of the way Serena recovered to 4-4 in the opening set but then sacrificed it with a wanton tenth game in which she not only double-faulted but ended it with an embarrassingly tame forehand tap over the sideline on the 19th stroke of the rally, having failed to put away a smash on the 11th.

Had this been in her quarter-final against Capriati, when she began so meekly, no-one would have blinked. Because it happened against Venus and settled the first set, it became a mountainous topic for debate.

Where Serena Williams had been unemotional in triumph on the Centre Court, Todd Woodbridge was far more appropriately animated as he demonstrated his delight at equalling the record for the most men's doubles titles at The Championships, a few hours

Todd Woodbridge safely makes a return in the men's doubles final which ended with his name on the trophy for a stunning eighth time and huge delight for him and Jonas Bjorkman as they retained the title.

& Bhupathi

later. Together with Jonas Bjorkman, with whom he had linked up a year earlier and immediately won the title by playing as if they had been together for years, Woodbridge's name went on the trophy for the eighth time, sharing the honour with the Doherty brothers, Hugh and Reggie, whose eighth success was recorded in 1905.

In what was frequently a quick-fire shoot-out for a large evening crowd on the Centre Court, long after all other matches were over for the day, the Australian and the equally talented Swede overcame the loss of the first set to beat top-seeded Max Mirnyi and Mahesh Bhupathi, 3-6, 6-3, 7-6 (7-4), 6-3.

Although immediately a break down, the Belarusian and the Indian, both already doubles champions at Wimbledon in earlier years, broke the Woodbridge serve in the fourth game but in the fifth game of the second set, Woodbridge and Bjorkman, combining skilfully, as well as enthusiastically, took Mirnyi's serve to lead 4-2 on their way to levelling the match.

The eventual winners crucially saved three break points against the Bjorkman serve to take the third set to a tie-break where, from 3-3, they pulled ahead and won the set with a Bjorkman smash and a typical take-that cut-off volley by Woodbridge. In the fourth set, a break point against the Woodbridge serve had to be clawed back but then the Mirnyi serve was broken and the 32-year-old Australian served out for the 76th title of his career, one fewer than John McEnroe and two behind the record holder, Tom Okker.

Whereas Martina Navratilova prefers tufts of the precious Centre Court grass as a keepsake, Woodbridge and Bjorkman settled for a ball each from the final batch in use to remind them of the day they will cherish far more than either of the Williams sisters.

Britain's interest in the junior competitions came to an end when Andrew Murray and Tom Rushby lost 6-3, 7-5 in the semi-finals to the Romanians, Florin Mergea and Horia Tecau, while Colin Dowdeswell and Buster Mottram lost to the American, formerly South African, pair Kevin Curren and Johan Kriek 6-3, 6-0 in the men's over-45 invitation doubles.

One for the family album. The Williams sisters persuaded All England Club Committee member, Geoff Newton, to photograph them with their own camera.

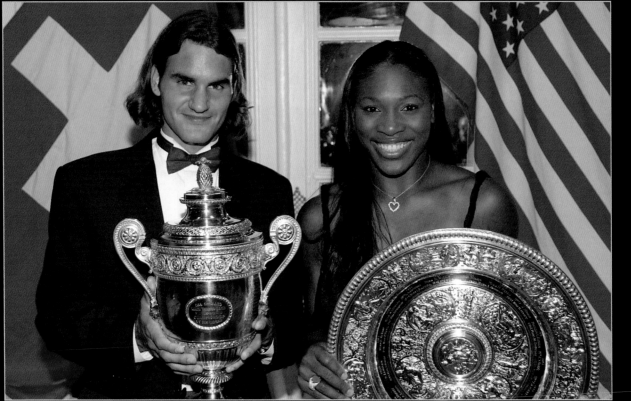

Take the ice-cool Wimbledon temperament of Bjorn Borg, add the elegant volleying skills of Stefan Edberg, stir with the serving authority of Pete Sampras and the returning qualities of Andre Agassi and there you have a taste of the 2003 Wimbledon champion, Roger Federer.

It took 21-year-old Federer only 1 hour 55 minutes to outclass Mark Philippoussis 7-6 (7-5), 6-2, 7-6 (7-3) to become the first Swiss winner of a men's Grand Slam title and only the third winner of the boys' title at The Championships in Open tennis to emulate that success in the men's singles after Borg and Edberg, memories of whom he had so brilliantly evoked.

Consequently, although it was not among the most dramatic finals, partly because Philippoussis's game faltered too often, no one surely, other than the most ardent fans of the Australian, especially those encamped on 'Henman Hill' — renamed 'Mark Mountain' for the day — was disappointed. The Centre Court crowd knew — and acknowledged as much by their prolonged standing ovation — that they had been witnessing an exceptional talent and a worthy champion.

No disrespect to the feisty, workman-like 2002 winner, Lleyton Hewitt, or the clay-court specialist, David Nalbandian, who occupied the Centre Court stage a year earlier, but this was a display much more to the taste of the tennis purist — enormous hitting, of course, but richly supplemented with Federer's inspiration, versatility, instinct and artistry.

Just as the opening day of Wimbledon 2003 had been memorable with Hewitt's first-round defeat by a 6ft 10in Croatian, Ivo Karlovic, so the final day reached a fitting climax with the triumph going to an amiable, thoughtful young man who could become a giant among champions.

At the moment of victory, Federer dropped to his knees, in the same fashion as Borg after each of his record five triumphs in succession. Only then did the nervous emotion that he had masked so effectively come to the surface. Two years after he had shed tears of joy when he ended Sampras's extraordinary reign of seven titles in eight years, in the fourth round, only then to lose to Tim Henman, so they flowed again.

He had overcome a fourth-round back injury which threatened to scupper his hopes, and dropped only one set — the best by any champion since Richard Krajicek in 1996 — and climbed to a career-best third in the world rankings.

Seldom has any champion — including Sampras, who brought his game to a similarly immaculate peak for his 1999 final against

Mark Philippoussis (opposite) fought hard to stay with Roger Federer (below) in the first set of the men's singles final.

Day 13 • Federer v Philippoussis

It was a proud moment for Nick Philippoussis (far left) watching his son on such a momentous occasion but early in the second set Roger Federer (below) began delivering those spectacular cross-court winners that were so significant in his triumph.

Agassi — maintained his ruthlessly impressive form in the semi-finals at the same almost-faultless level in the final.

The sentimental support was with Philippoussis, simply because of the well known mental and physical stress he had suffered in recent times. Sentiment, though, does not win matches, especially a Wimbledon final.

Nor did he help himself though, for, crucially, there were moments of impetuosity that cost him the mini-breaks he had established on the opening point of both tie-breaks and he never looked like being good enough to stop an opponent riding serenely towards the achievement of a lifelong dream.

Federer fell in love not only with the unique, captivating atmosphere of Wimbledon as a junior but realised from day one that ultimately it could prove to be the best surface for his stylish, subtle and skilfully well-rounded game.

One of the keys to the final was always going to be how well Federer would cope not so much with the Philippoussis first serve, but also the Australian's second serve which in his quarter-final recovery from two sets down against Germany's equally unseeded Alexander Popp and his semi-final against Grosjean so often came to the rescue with deliveries in excess of 125 mph.

The young man from Basle, who flew home in a private plane to a hero's welcome in Gstaad where he would keep his promise to compete in the Swiss Open, watched by sell-out crowds, was steadfastly unperturbed. He switched between full-blooded and blocked returns with almost as much reward as against Andy Roddick two days earlier as he completed his 50th match win of the year, and his fifth title of the year on four different surfaces — his second on grass.

The transformation from the previous year, when Federer lost to qualifier Mario Ancic in the first round, was complete, though not really unexpected. Although he had lost enough major matches for some to wonder if he would ever have the belief to conquer the biggest occasions, his exceptional abilities left one convinced that it was still only a matter of when, rather than if, he would scale the game's most important peak.

Perhaps most significantly Federer and his astute coach, Peter Lundgren, always believed winning Wimbledon was possible, although as the new champion put it 'When it happens, you don't think it is possible. It's something I cannot even understand yet because it's just too good.'

As the naturally disappointed Philippoussis said, the tie-break at the end of the first set was vital. Apart from his initial mini-break, he had another to put him 4-3 ahead but missed a forehand and then went for too much on a second serve and double-faulted. 'I knew that whoever won that first set was gonna go on a roll and get more confident', he said.

He was spot on. Federer, solid as a rock in mood and deed, broke in the first and third games of the second set not so much because the Philippoussis serve was faltering but by producing great passing shots, running forehands and cunning backhand returns. 'What can you do?' Philippoussis asked forlornly after only once getting to deuce on the silky smooth Federer serve.

Federer's supremacy was underlined by the statistics, 21 aces to the 14 by Philippoussis, whose total for seven matches increased to 178. Even more spectacular was Federer's tally of 50 winners and a mere nine unforced errors compared with the Australian's more than respectable totals of 37-13.

Although some of the impetus went from Federer's game for a while early in the third set his authority was never seriously threatened. The aces or winning serves and the rasping forehands were still there when they were required and after again sacrificing an early mini-break in the tie-break he raced away to 6-1 with the ease of Switzerland's triumph in the America's Cup. Philippoussis saved two match points but then netted a backhand service return. 'He was too good,' he said of Federer.

Good too for Wimbledon and for tennis, he might have added.

That night at The Champion's Dinner, Federer recalled how he should have been there after his junior success in 1998 but, on the advice of his former coach, Peter Carter, tragically killed in a road accident in 2001, he turned down the invitation because Gstaad

had granted him a wild card into what was to be his first tournament on the ATP Tour and in true professional style 'he wanted to prepare as well as possible.'

'Looking back,' he said, 'that was maybe a mistake but I'm thrilled I've had a second chance. It's always been my dream to win Wimbledon, there's such a special magic about the place. I'm proud to have become a member of The All England Club.'

Apart from Federer, no player enjoyed Wimbledon 2003 more than Martina Navratilova, who was given her own round of applause when she arrived at The Champions' Dinner, even before the official congratulations offered when the reigning and many past champions were introduced by Tim Phillips, the Chairman of The All England Club.

At the ripe old age of 46 and no less than 30 years since she first stepped onto the grass at Wimbledon, she brought this year's Championships to an emotional, historic climax by claiming a share in Billie Jean King's record of 20 titles, established in 1979. The last of King's titles had been earned with Navratilova as her partner in the ladies' doubles, just a year after the finest woman player the game has known had won the first of her record nine singles crowns.

This latest success, which left her pining for even more, came as she partnered Leander Paes to 6-3, 6-3 triumph over the unseeded Israeli Andy Ram and the Russian, Anastasia Rodionova, watched by a packed Centre Court excitedly convinced that there would be a happy ending. When Paes put away a smash on match point as he served out the match to love, he bowed in thanks to his illustrious partner, who shed tears as she collapsed into his arms.

Still wiping her eyes, she told the crowd 'All Wimbledon titles are special but the last one was eight years ago so it's great to bridge such a long gap with this very, very special

The emotion was almost too much for Roger Federer (left) as he achieved a lifetime's dream.

Below: The irrepressible Martina Navratilova was the Centre Court heroine yet again as she won the mixed doubles title with Leander Paes to equal Billie Jean King's record.

Over the fortnight, The Championships attracted a total attendance of 470,802, the second highest in the tournament's history. This included daily records on the first Tuesday and first Thursday. More than 5000 hours of television coverage were transmitted to approximately 1.8 billion people across 160 countries, with the BBC viewing figures in Britain peaking at 12.7 million during Tim Henman's fourth-round match against David Nalbandian.

Compensation for Kim Clijsters (below) as she wins the ladies' doubles crown with Ai Sugiyama.

honour.' Then to another burst of cheering, she added 'I'll be back next year but I don't know in what capacity.'

There were smiles too from Kim Clijsters and Japan's Ai Sugiyama as they added the Wimbledon ladies' doubles title to that of the French Open they had won a month earlier, also in a final against top seeds Virginia Ruano Pascual and Paola Suarez. The score was 6-4, 6-4.

Added to Clijster's delight was the success of fellow Belgian, Kirsten Flipkens, in the final of the junior girls' singles. Flipkens, who plays doubles with Clijster's younger sister, Elke, hurled herself face down into the grass on Number Two Court, as a second serve from the Russian, Anna Tchakvetadze, finished halfway up the net on match point. Flipkens then draped herself in the Belgian flag for the presentation and blew kisses to her enthusiastic supporters, who a day earlier for her semi-final on a packed Number One Court had also included Clijsters, Lleyton Hewitt and Hewitt's parents, Glynn and Cherilyn.

Romanians were also celebrating. Florin Mergea not only won the boys' singles, beating Australia's Chris Guccione 6-2, 7-6 (7-3) but then became the first to win the doubles title as well in the same year since Federer in 1998, when he partnered fellow countryman, Horia Tecau, to a 7-6 (7-4), 7-5 win over Guccione and another Australian, Adam Feeney.

Richard Krajicek's half-sister, Michaela Krajicek, missed out on adding to the family silver when she and Katerina Bohmova from the Czech Republic were beaten 6-2, 6-3, 6-2 in the final of the girls' doubles by Russia's Alisa Kleybanova and Indian, Sania Mirza, playing their first tournament together.

Finally, there was some compensation for British tennis. Although Jo Durie and the American, Gretchen Magers, were beaten 4-6, 6-4, 5-7 in the final of the women's 35-and-over invitation doubles by Ilana Kloss and Kathy Rinaldi, Jeremy Bates and Nick Fulwood took the equivalent 45-and-over men's title, 6-2, 6-4 against Gary Wayne Donnelly and Luke Jensen.

Roll on, Wimbledon 2004!

Junior girls' singles

The roll of honour among the juniors: Kirsten Flipkens (top left) who beat Anna Tchakvetadze, and Florin Mergea (left), winner against Chris Guccione.

The Gentlemen's Singles Championship

Roger Federer

The Ladies' Singles Championship

Serena Williams

The Gentlemen's Doubles Championship

Jonas Bjorkman & Todd Woodbridge

The Mixed Doubles Championship

Leander Paes & Martina Navratilova

The Ladies' Doubles Championship

Kim Klijsters & Ai Sugiyama

The 35 and over Ladies' Invitation Doubles

Ilana Kloss & Kathy Rinaldi

The Girls' Doubles Championship

Alisa Kleybanova & Sania Mirza

The Boys' Doubles Championship

Horia Tecau & Florin Mergea

The Girls' Singles Championship

Kirsten Flipkens

The Boys' Singles Championship

Florin Mergea

The 45 and over Gentlemen's Invitation Doubles

Kevin Curren & Johan Kriek

The 35 and over Gentlemen's Invitation Doubles

Nick Fulwood & Jeremy Bates

CHAMPIONSHIP
RECORDS
2003

ALPHABETICAL LIST OF COMPETITORS

LADIES

114 Ahl Miss L.A. *(Great Britain)*
Arendt Miss N. *(USA)*
78 Asagoe Miss S. *(Japan)*
Ashley Miss T. *(USA)*
Augustus Miss A. *(USA)*
50 Baltacha Miss E. *(Great Britain)*
Barclay Miss C. *(Australia)*
111 Barna Miss A. *(Germany)*
79 Bartoli Miss M. *(France)*
117 Bedanova Miss D. *(Czech Republic)*
28 Benesova Miss I. *(Czech Republic)*
Beygelzimer Miss Y. *(Ukraine)*
63 Bielik Miss B. *(USA)*
69 Black Miss C. *(Zimbabwe)*
Boogert Miss K. *(Netherlands)*
Borwell Miss S. *(Great Britain)*
56 Bovina Miss E. *(Russia)*
3 Callens Miss E.S.H. *(Belgium)*
60 Camerin Miss M. *(Italy)*
32 Capriati Miss J. *(USA)*
46 Cargill Miss A. *(USA)*
31 Casanova Miss M. *(Switzerland)*
115 Cervanova Miss L. *(Slovak Republic)*
72 Chladkova Miss D. *(Czech Republic)*
62 Cho Miss Y.J. *(Korea Republic)*
128 Clijsters Miss K. *(Belgium)*
73 Coetzer Miss A.J. *(South Africa)*
52 Cohen Aloro Miss S. *(France)*
2 Craybas Miss J. *(USA)*
Crook Miss H. *(Great Britain)*
48 Daniilidou Miss E. *(Greece)*
65 Davenport Miss L. *(USA)*
De Villiers Miss N. *(South Africa)*
120 Dechy Miss N. *(France)*
Dekmeijere Miss L. *(Latvia)*
16 Dementieva Miss E. *(Russia)*
Dhenin Miss C. *(France)*
49 Dokic Miss J. *(Yugoslavia)*
82 Dominikovic Miss E. *(Australia)*
Dragomir Ilie Mrs R. *(Romania)*
102 Drake Miss M. *(Canada)*
Dulko Miss G. *(Argentina)*
Embry Miss J. *(USA)*
104 Farina Elia Mrs S. *(Italy)*
124 Fernandez Miss C. *(Argentina)*
116 Fislova Miss E. *(Slovak Republic)*
42 Foretz Miss S. *(France)*
100 Frazier Miss A. *(USA)*
Freye Miss K. *(Germany)*
Fujiwara Miss R. *(Japan)*
51 Gagliardi Miss E. *(Switzerland)*
90 Garbin Miss T. *(Italy)*
67 Grande Miss R. *(Italy)*
Grandin Miss N. *(South Africa)*
8 Granville Miss L. *(USA)*
85 Gullickson Miss C. *(USA)*
80 Hantuchova Miss D. *(Slovak Republic)*
54 Harkleroad Miss A. *(USA)*
Hawkins Miss A. *(Great Britain)*
33 Henin-Hardenne Mrs J. *(Belgium)*
95 Hrozenska Miss S. *(Slovak Republic)*
Huber Mrs L. *(South Africa)*
119 Husarova Miss J. *(Slovak Republic)*
29 Irvin Miss M. *(USA)*
Janes Miss A. *(Great Britain)*
Jeyaseelan Miss S. *(Canada)*
7 Jidkova Miss A. *(Russia)*
10 Kapros Miss A. *(Hungary)*
93 Keothavong Miss A. *(Great Britain)*
70 Kleinova Miss S. *(Czech Republic)*
47 Kostanic Miss J. *(Croatia)*
71 Koukalova Miss K. *(Czech Republic)*
91 Koulikovskaya Miss E. *(Russia)*
19 Krasnoroutskaya Miss L. *(Russia)*
Krizan Miss T. *(Slovenia)*
64 Kuznetsova Miss S. *(Russia)*
Lamade Miss B. *(Germany)*
77 Lee Miss J. *(Chinese Taipei)*
39 Lee-Waters Mrs L. *(USA)*
11 Leon Garcia Miss G. *(Spain)*
40 Likhovtseva Miss E. *(Russia)*
58 Loit Miss E. *(France)*
98 Majoli Miss I. *(Croatia)*
112 Maleeva Miss M. *(Bulgaria)*
87 Mandula Miss P. *(Hungary)*
Marosi Miss K. *(Hungary)*
22 Marrero Miss M. *(Spain)*
24 Martinez Miss C. *(Spain)*
83 Martinez Granados Miss C. *(Spain)*
108 Matevzic Miss M. *(Slovenia)*
McQuillan Miss R. *(Australia)*
McShea Miss L. *(Australia)*
30 Mikaelian Miss M-G. *(Switzerland)*
Miyagi Miss N. *(Japan)*
38 Molik Miss A. *(Australia)*
35 Morariu Miss C. *(USA)*
26 Morigami Miss A. *(Japan)*
Muller Miss M. *(Germany)*
Musgrave Miss T. *(Australia)*
17 Myskina Miss A. *(Russia)*
18 Nagyova Miss H. *(Slovak Republic)*
Navratilova Miss M. *(USA)*
127 Neffa-De Los Rios Mrs R. *(Paraguay)*
75 Noorlander Miss S. *(Netherlands)*
43 O'Donoghue Miss J. *(Great Britain)*
55 Obata Miss S. *(Japan)*
14 Ondraskova Miss Z. *(Czech Republic)*
59 Osterloh Miss L. *(USA)*
13 Parra Miss A. *(Spain)*
36 Pennetta Miss F. *(Italy)*
6 Perebiynis Miss T. *(Ukraine)*
89 Petrova Miss N. *(Russia)*
45 Pierce Miss M. *(France)*
107 Pisnik Miss T. *(Slovenia)*
121 Pistolesi Mrs A. *(Israel)*
118 Poutchek Miss T. *(Belarus)*
Prakusya Miss W. *(Indonesia)*
101 Pratt Miss N.J. *(Australia)*
20 Pullin Miss J.M. *(Great Britain)*
74 Randriantefy Miss D. *(Madagascar)*
41 Raymond Miss L.M. *(USA)*
125 Razzano Miss V. *(France)*
122 Reeves Miss S. *(USA)*
4 Rittner Miss B. *(Germany)*
126 Rodionova Miss A. *(Russia)*
15 Roesch Miss A. *(Germany)*
106 Ruano Pascual Miss V. *(Spain)*
97 Rubin Miss C. *(USA)*
37 Safina Miss D. *(Russia)*
Salerni Miss M. *(Argentina)*
103 Sanchez Lorenzo Miss M. *(Spain)*
21 Schett Miss B. *(Austria)*
76 Schiavone Miss F. *(Italy)*
88 Schnyder Miss P. *(Switzerland)*
Selyutina Miss I. *(Kazakhstan)*
23 Sequera Miss M. *(Venezuela)*
105 Serna Miss M. *(Spain)*
Serra Zanetti Miss A. *(Italy)*
84 Serra Zanetti Miss A. *(Italy)*
Sewell Miss N. *(Australia)*
110 Sfar Miss S. *(Tunisia)*
53 Sharapova Miss M. *(Russia)*
9 Shaughnessy Miss M. *(USA)*
Spears Miss A. *(USA)*
27 Sprem Miss K. *(Croatia)*
94 Srebotnik Miss K. *(Slovenia)*
57 Stevenson Miss A. *(USA)*
Stewart Miss B. *(Australia)*
Stone Miss S. *(Australia)*
66 Stosur Miss S. *(Australia)*
5 Strycova Miss B. *(Czech Republic)*
Stubbs Miss R.P. *(Australia)*
109 Suarez Miss P. *(Argentina)*
12 Sucha Miss M. *(Slovak Republic)*
113 Sugiyama Miss A. *(Japan)*
99 Talaja Miss S. *(Croatia)*
25 Tanasugarn Miss T. *(Thailand)*
Tarabini Miss P. *(Argentina)*
Tatarkova Miss E. *(Ukraine)*
61 Torrens Valero Miss C. *(Spain)*
Tu Miss M. *(USA)*
86 Tulyaganova Miss I. *(Uzbekhistan)*
34 Vakulenko Miss J. *(Ukraine)*
Vanc Miss A. *(Romania)*
Vento-Kabchi Mrs M. *(Venezuela)*
Vinci Miss R. *(Italy)*
Vis Miss C.M. *(Netherlands)*
Voracova Miss R. *(Czech Republic)*
68 Wartusch Miss P. *(Austria)*
Washington Miss M. *(USA)*
Webb Miss V. *(Canada)*
44 Weingartner Miss M. *(Germany)*
Wheeler Miss C. *(Australia)*
92 Widjaja Miss A. *(Indonesia)*
1 Williams Miss S. *(USA)*
96 Williams Miss V. *(USA)*
123 Zuluaga Miss F. *(Colombia)*
81 Zvonareva Miss V. *(Russia)*

GENTLEMEN

26 Acasuso J. *(Argentina)*
Adams D. *(South Africa)*
128 Agassi A. *(USA)*
22 Ancic M. *(Croatia)*
107 Arazi H. *(Morocco)*
Arnold L. *(Argentina)*
84 Arthurs W. *(Australia)*
Aspelin S. *(Sweden)*
Auckland J. *(Great Britain)*
4 Baccanello P. *(Australia)*
47 Beck K. *(Slovak Republic)*
58 Behrend T. *(Germany)*
Bertolini M. *(Italy)*
Bhupathi M. *(India)*
12 Bjorkman J. *(Sweden)*
Black W. *(Zimbabwe)*
89 Blake J. *(USA)*
99 Bloomfield R. *(Great Britain)*
92 Bogdanovic A. *(Great Britain)*
102 Boutter J. *(France)*
Bowen D. *(USA)*
Bryan B. *(USA)*
Bryan M. *(USA)*
125 Burgsmuller L. *(Germany)*
41 Calleri A. *(Argentina)*
61 Carlsen K. *(Denmark)*
Carrasco J. *(Spain)*
Cermak F. *(Czech Republic)*
57 Chela J.I. *(Argentina)*
23 Childs L. *(Great Britain)*
Chiudinelli M. *(Switzerland)*
Cibulec T. *(Czech Republic)*
16 Clement A. *(France)*
97 Coria G. *(Argentina)*
Crabb J. *(Australia)*
Damm M. *(Czech Republic)*
24 Davydenko N. *(Russia)*
De Jager J-L. *(South Africa)*
127 Delgado J. *(Great Britain)*
5 Dent T. *(USA)*
117 Draper S. *(Australia)*
100 Dupuis A. *(France)*
Eagle J. *(Australia)*
94 Economidis K. *(Greece)*
121 El Aynaoui Y. *(Morocco)*
75 Elseneer G. *(Belgium)*
82 Enqvist T. *(Sweden)*
Erlich J. *(Israel)*
93 Escude N. *(France)*
Etlis G. *(Argentina)*
33 Federer R. *(Switzerland)*
72 Ferreira W. *(South Africa)*
109 Ferrer D. *(Spain)*
96 Ferrero J.C. *(Spain)*
39 Fish M. *(USA)*
Fisher A. *(Australia)*
Freelove O. *(Great Britain)*
Friedl L. *(Czech Republic)*
Fukarek O. *(Czech Republic)*
101 Galvani S. *(Italy)*
37 Gambill J-M. *(USA)*
Garcia M. *(Argentina)*
40 Gaudio G. *(Argentina)*
14 Gimelstob J. *(USA)*
15 Ginepri R. *(USA)*
9 Gonzalez F. *(Chile)*
81 Grosjean S. *(France)*
Haarhuis P. *(Netherlands)*
Hadad A. *(Israel)*
Haggard C. *(South Africa)*
59 Hanescu V. *(Romania)*
Hanley P. *(Australia)*
Healey N. *(Australia)*
80 Henman T. *(Great Britain)*
3 Heuberger I. *(Switzerland)*
1 Hewitt L. *(Australia)*
122 Hilton M.A. *(Great Britain)*
Hood M. *(Argentina)*
111 Horna L. *(Peru)*
18 Hrbaty D. *(Slovak Republic)*
Humphries S. *(USA)*
Huss S. *(Australia)*
Johnson D. *(USA)*
105 Kafelnikov Y. *(Russia)*
2 Karlovic I. *(Croatia)*
46 Kendrick R. *(USA)*
Kerr J. *(Australia)*
76 Kiefer N. *(Germany)*
Knowle J. *(Austria)*
Knowles M. *(Bahamas)*
Koenig R. *(South Africa)*
35 Koubek S. *(Austria)*
123 Krajan Z. *(Croatia)*
50 Kratochvil M. *(Switzerland)*
Kratzmann A. *(Australia)*
71 Kucera K. *(Slovak Republic)*
56 Kuerten G. *(Brazil)*
38 Kunitsyn I. *(Russia)*
13 Labadze I. *(Georgia)*
Landsberg J. *(Sweden)*
Lapentti G. *(Ecuador)*
62 Lapentti N. *(Ecuador)*
90 Larkham T. *(Australia)*
Leach R. *(USA)*
34 Lee H-T. *(Korea Republic)*
110 Lee M. *(Great Britain)*
95 Lisnard J-R. *(France)*
6 Ljubicic I. *(Croatia)*
78 Llodra M. *(France)*
45 Lopez F. *(Spain)*
Lopez Moron A. *(Spain)*
Luczak P. *(Australia)*
11 Luxa P. *(Czech Republic)*
44 Mackin A.R. *(Great Britain)*
MacLagan M. *(Great Britain)*
MacPhie B. *(USA)*
113 Malisse X. *(Belgium)*
88 Mantilla F. *(Spain)*
Marray J. *(Great Britain)*
83 Martin A. *(Spain)*
54 Martin T. *(USA)*
124 Massu N. *(Chile)*
118 Mathieu P-H. *(France)*
10 Melzer J. *(Austria)*
Merklein M. *(Bahamas)*
119 Mertinak M. *(Slovak Republic)*
7 Mirnyi M. *(Belarus)*
126 Montanes A. *(Spain)*
85 Moodie W. *(South Africa)*
19 Mutis O. *(France)*
21 Nadal R. *(Spain)*
65 Nalbandian D. *(Argentina)*
Nestor D. *(Canada)*
87 Niemeyer F. *(Canada)*
104 Nieminen J. *(Finland)*
69 Norman D. *(Belgium)*
112 Novak J. *(Czech Republic)*
Olhovskiy A. *(Russia)*
Oliver G. *(USA)*
Paes L. *(India)*
Pala P. *(Czech Republic)*
Palmer J. *(USA)*
63 Parmar A. *(Great Britain)*
Perry T. *(Australia)*
116 Philippoussis M. *(Australia)*
108 Popp A. *(Germany)*
60 Portas A. *(Spain)*
Prieto S. *(Argentina)*
Prinosil D. *(Germany)*
68 Puerta M. *(Argentina)*
Qureshi A-U-H. *(Pakistan)*
Ram A. *(Israel)*
Rikl D. *(Czech Republic)*
25 Robredo T. *(Spain)*
36 Rochus C. *(Belgium)*
98 Rochus O. *(Belgium)*
32 Roddick A. *(USA)*
Rodriguez M. *(Argentina)*
Roitman S. *(Argentina)*
Ross A. *(Australia)*
86 Rosset M. *(Switzerland)*
30 Rusedski G. *(Great Britain)*
67 Sa A. *(Brazil)*
77 Sanchez D. *(Spain)*
31 Sanguinetti D. *(Italy)*
52 Santoro F. *(France)*
43 Saretta F. *(Brazil)*
91 Sargsian S. *(Armenia)*
114 Saulnier C. *(France)*
64 Schalken S. *(Netherlands)*
Schneiter A. *(Argentina)*
49 Schuettler R. *(Germany)*
Sherwood D. *(Great Britain)*
Shimada T. *(Japan)*
Skoch D. *(Czech Republic)*
106 Sluiter R. *(Netherlands)*
74 Soderling R. *(Sweden)*
8 Spadea V. *(USA)*
20 Squillari F. *(Argentina)*
17 Srichaphan P. *(Thailand)*
120 Stepanek R. *(Czech Republic)*
Suk C. *(Czech Republic)*
70 Suzuki T. *(Japan)*
Tarango J. *(USA)*
Thomas J. *(USA)*
Ullyett K. *(Zimbabwe)*
Vacek D. *(Czech Republic)*
27 Vahaly B. *(USA)*
55 Van Lottum J. *(Netherlands)*
Vanhoudt T. *(Belgium)*
103 Verdasco F. *(Spain)*
73 Verkerk M. *(Netherlands)*
53 Vicente F. *(Spain)*
51 Vinciguerra A. *(Sweden)*
Vizner P. *(Czech Republic)*
42 Voinea A. *(Romania)*
28 Volandri F. *(Italy)*
66 Voltchkov V. *(Belarus)*
Wakefield M. *(South Africa)*
29 Waske A. *(Germany)*
Woodbridge T.A. *(Australia)*
48 Youzhny M. *(Russia)*
115 Zabaleta M. *(Argentina)*
79 Zib T. *(Czech Republic)*
Zimonjic N. *(Yugoslavia)*
Zovko L. *(Croatia)*

GIRLS

3 Andersson Miss M. *(Sweden)*
35 Babos Miss Z. *(Hungary)*
4 Bacsinszky Miss T. *(Switzerland)*
43 Bagshaw Miss H. *(Great Britain)*
33 Baker Miss A. *(USA)*
27 Baker Miss K. *(Great Britain)*
36 Bhambri Miss S. *(India)*
49 Bohmova Miss K. *(Czech Republic)*
21 Bondarenko Miss K. *(Ukraine)*
13 Bunic Miss T. *(Croatia)*
26 Cohen Miss J. *(USA)*
30 Corovic Miss V. *(Yugoslavia)*
47 Czafikova Miss K. *(Slovak Republic)*
24 Dellacqua Miss C. *(Australia)*
41 Domachowska Miss M. *(Poland)*
29 Du Miss R. *(China P.R.)*
15 Dubois Miss S. *(Canada)*
54 El Tabakh Miss H. *(Egypt)*
23 Falcon Miss M. *(USA)*
55 Ferguson Miss S. *(Australia)*
14 Flipkens Miss K. *(Belgium)*
32 Fuda Miss R. *(Japan)*
17 Gajdosova Miss J. *(Slovak Republic)*
28 Giltinan Miss L. *(Australia)*
51 Gojnea Miss M. *(Romania)*
25 Golovin Miss T. *(France)*
18 Gonzalez Penas Miss A. *(Spain)*
34 Grady Miss H. *(Great Britain)*
64 Gullickson Miss C. *(USA)*
39 Havartsova Miss V. *(Belarus)*
9 Hlavackova Miss A. *(Czech Republic)*
31 Ichim Miss I. *(USA)*
12 Ivanovic Miss A. *(Yugoslavia)*
62 Kawatoko Miss M. *(Japan)*
58 Kerber Miss A. *(Germany)*
16 Kleybanova Miss A. *(Russia)*
44 Ko Miss B. *(Canada)*
48 Krajicek Miss M. *(Netherlands)*
59 Kudryavtseva Miss A. *(Russia)*
57 Kutuzova Miss V. *(Ukraine)*
56 Laine Miss E. *(Finland)*
40 Lukic Miss V. *(Yugoslavia)*
5 Marama Miss E. *(New Zealand)*
22 Marcio Miss K. *(USA)*
8 Mirza Miss S. *(India)*
46 Mitchell Miss M. *(USA)*
11 Moulton-Levy Miss M. *(USA)*
50 O'Brien Miss K. *(Great Britain)*
38 Pavic Miss N. *(Croatia)*
37 Peer Miss S. *(Israel)*
10 Peterzan Miss C. *(Great Britain)*
1 Rao Miss S. *(USA)*
19 Rudman Miss T. *(South Africa)*
45 Safarova Miss L. *(Czech Republic)*
52 Smolenakova Miss L. *(Slovak Republic)*
63 Stoop Miss G. *(Great Britain)*
60 Sun Miss S-N. *(China P.R.)*
2 Szavay Miss A. *(Hungary)*
Szili Miss A. *(Australia)*
6 Tangphong Miss M. *(Thailand)*
42 Tchakvetadze Miss A. *(Russia)*
7 Tsutskova Miss A. *(Ukraine)*
31 Vaidisova Miss N. *(Czech Republic)*
61 Vitayaviroj Miss T. *(Thailand)*
20 Zoricic Miss K. *(Canada)*

BOYS

30 Abid H. *(Tunisia)*
13 Amado J. *(Argentina)*
50 Arevalo Gonzalez R. *(El Salvador)*
64 Baker B. *(USA)*
58 Baker J. *(Great Britain)*
33 Balazs G. *(Hungary)*
1 Berdych T. *(Czech Republic)*
24 Brewer D. *(Great Britain)*
52 Brown M. *(Great Britain)*
31 Burn T. *(Great Britain)*
53 Cameron R. *(USA)*
21 Chikhladze L. *(Georgia)*
26 Chirico J. *(USA)*
5 Cuellar J. *(El Salvador)*
36 Dev Varman S. *(India)*
45 Evans B. *(USA)*
23 Fass A. *(USA)*
3 Feeney A. *(Australia)*
51 Figueroa P. *(Sweden)*
22 Flores L. *(Mexico)*
61 Fognini F. *(Italy)*
41 Gil F. *(Portugal)*
56 Gimeno-Traver D. *(Spain)*
6 Goodall J. *(Great Britain)*
49 Guccione C. *(Australia)*
44 Hadzic T. *(Croatia)*
60 Huta-Galung J. *(Netherlands)*
42 Hutchins R. *(Great Britain)*
46 Irwin R. *(Great Britain)*
19 Jarc R. *(Slovenia)*
12 Kasiri M. *(Great Britain)*
47 Kim S-Y. *(Korea Republic)*
57 Kirche L. *(Brazil)*
27 Kravchuk K. *(Russia)*
7 Kuznetsov A. *(USA)*
25 Kwon C. *(USA)*
43 Lowe M. *(Great Britain)*
16 Mergea F. *(Romania)*
55 Monfils G. *(France)*
48 Montcourt M. *(France)*
11 Muguruza J.L. *(Aruba)*
15 Muller D. *(Germany)*
35 Mullings D. *(Bahamas)*
40 Murray A. *(Great Britain)*
4 Ouanna J. *(France)*
10 Oudsema S. *(USA)*
18 Rastogi K. *(India)*
54 Rieschick S. *(Germany)*
9 Rosa B. *(Brazil)*
Rushby T. *(Great Britain)*
17 Sela D. *(Israel)*
38 Simmonds P. *(USA)*
37 Smeets R. *(Australia)*
63 Stakhovsky S. *(Ukraine)*
39 Steinberger P. *(Germany)*
8 Suk H-J. *(Korea Republic)*
14 Tatuhey R. *(Netherlands)*
34 Tecau H. *(Romania)*
29 Thomas G. *(Great Britain)*
32 Tsonga J-W. *(France)*
28 Ungur A. *(Romania)*
2 Weber A. *(Germany)*
62 Wolmarans F. *(South Africa)*
59 Zivkovic D. *(USA)*
20 Zverev M. *(Germany)*

Bold figures denote position in Singles Draw

The winner becomes the holder, for the year only, of the CHALLENGE CUP presented by The All England Lawn Tennis and Croquet Club. The winner receives a silver replica of the Challenge Cup. A silver salver is presented to the runner-up and a bronze medal to each defeated semi-finalist.

Heavy type denotes seeded players. The figure in brackets against names denotes the order in which they have been seeded. (W) = Wild card. (Q) = Qualifier. (L) = Lucky loser.

The matches are the best of five sets

THE GENTLEMEN'S DOUBLES CHAMPIONSHIP

Holders: J Bjorkman and T A Woodbridge

The winners become the holders, for the year only, of the CHALLENGE CUPS presented by the OXFORD UNIVERSITY LAWN TENNIS CLUB and the late SIR HERBERT WILBERFORCE respectively. The winners receive silver replicas of the two Challenge Cups. A silver salver is presented to each of the runners-up, and a bronze medal to each defeated semi-finalist.

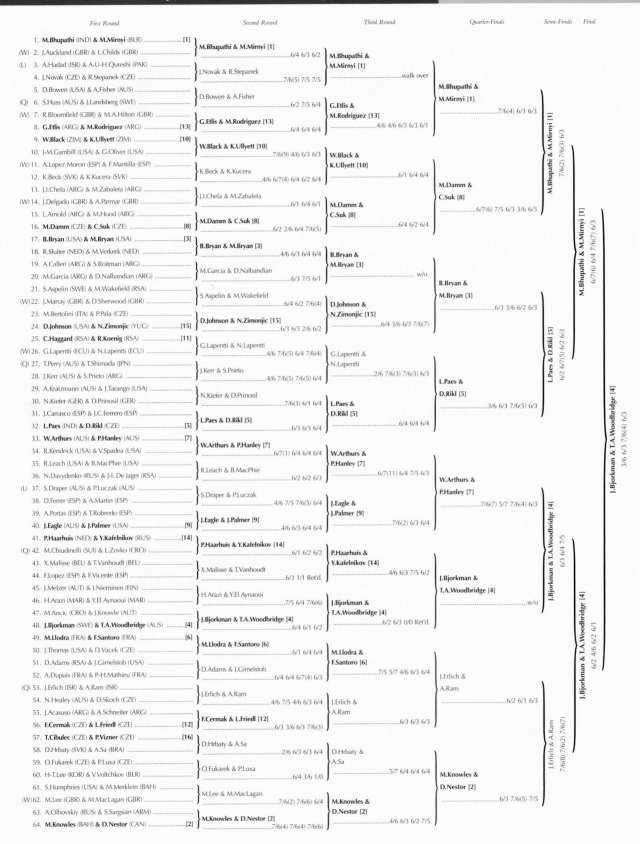

	First Round	Second Round	Third Round	Quarter-Finals	Semi-Finals	Final

1. **M.Bhupathi** (IND) & **M.Mirnyi** (BLR) ....[1]
(W) 2. J.Auckland (GBR) & L.Childs (GBR)
M.Bhupathi & M.Mirnyi [1] 6/4 6/3 6/2
(L) 3. A.Hadad (ISR) & A-U-H.Qureshi (PAK)
4. J.Novak (CZE) & R.Stepanek (CZE)
J.Novak & R.Stepanek ....7/6(5) 7/5 7/5
M.Bhupathi & M.Mirnyi [1] ....walk over
5. D.Bowen (USA) & A.Fisher (AUS)
(Q) 6. S.Huss (AUS) & J.Landsberg (SWE)
D.Bowen & A.Fisher 6/2 7/5 6/4
(W) 7. R.Bloomfield (GBR) & M.A.Hilton (GBR)
8. **G.Etlis** (ARG) & **M.Rodriguez** (ARG) ....[13]
G.Etlis & M.Rodriguez [13] 6/4 6/4 6/4
G.Etlis & M.Rodriguez [13] 4/6 4/6 6/3 6/3 6/1
M.Bhupathi & M.Mirnyi [1] ....7/6(4) 6/3 6/3
9. **W.Black** (ZIM) & **K.Ullyett** (ZIM) ....[10]
10. J-M.Gambill (USA) & G.Oliver (USA)
W.Black & K.Ullyett [10] ....7/6(9) 4/6 6/3 6/3
(W) 11. A.Lopez Moron (ESP) & F.Mantilla (ESP)
12. K.Beck (SVK) & K.Kucera (SVK)
K.Beck & K.Kucera ....4/6 6/7(4) 6/4 6/2 6/4
W.Black & K.Ullyett [10] 6/1 6/4 6/4
13. J.I.Chela (ARG) & M.Zabaleta (ARG)
(W) 14. J.Delgado (GBR) & A.Parmar (GBR)
J.I.Chela & M.Zabaleta 6/1 6/4 6/1
M.Damm & C.Suk [8] 6/4 6/2 6/4
15. L.Arnold (ARG) & M.Hood (ARG)
16. **M.Damm** (CZE) & **C.Suk** (CZE) ....[8]
M.Damm & C.Suk [8] ....6/2 2/6 6/4 7/6(5)
M.Damm & C.Suk [8] ....6/7(6) 7/5 6/3 3/6 6/3

17. **B.Bryan** (USA) & **M.Bryan** (USA) ....[3]
18. R.Sluiter (NED) & M.Verkerk (NED)
B.Bryan & M.Bryan [3] 4/6 6/3 6/4 6/4
19. A.Calleri (ARG) & S.Roitman (ARG)
20. M.Garcia (ARG) & D.Nalbandian (ARG)
M.Garcia & D.Nalbandian 6/3 7/5 6/1
B.Bryan & M.Bryan [3] ....w/o
21. S.Aspelin (SWE) & M.Wakefield (RSA)
(W) 22. J.Marray (GBR) & D.Sherwood (GBR)
S.Aspelin & M.Wakefield ....6/4 6/2 7/6(4)
B.Bryan & M.Bryan [3] 6/3 3/6 6/2 6/3
23. M.Bertolini (ITA) & P.Pala (CZE)
24. **D.Johnson** (USA) & **N.Zimonjic** (YUG) ....[15]
D.Johnson & N.Zimonjic [15] 6/3 6/3 2/6 6/2
D.Johnson & N.Zimonjic [15] ....6/4 3/6 6/3 7/6(7)
25. **C.Haggard** (RSA) & **R.Koenig** (RSA) ....[11]
(W) 26. G.Lapentti (ECU) & N.Lapentti (ECU)
G.Lapentti & N.Lapentti ....4/6 7/6(5) 6/4 7/6(4)
G.Lapentti & N.Lapentti ....2/6 7/6(3) 7/6(3) 6/3
L.Paes & D.Rikl [5] ....6/2 6/7(5) 6/2 6/3
(Q) 27. T.Perry (AUS) & T.Shimada (JPN)
28. J.Kerr (AUS) & S.Prieto (ARG)
J.Kerr & S.Prieto ....4/6 7/6(5) 7/6(5) 6/4
L.Paes & D.Rikl [5] ....3/6 6/3 7/6(5) 6/3
29. A.Kratzmann (AUS) & J.Tarango (USA)
30. N.Kiefer (GER) & D.Prinosil (GER)
N.Kiefer & D.Prinosil ....7/6(3) 6/1 6/4
L.Paes & D.Rikl [5] 6/4 6/4 6/4
31. J.Carrasco (ESP) & J.C.Ferrero (ESP)
32. **L.Paes** (IND) & **D.Rikl** (CZE) ....[5]
L.Paes & D.Rikl [5] 6/3 6/3 6/4

33. **W.Arthurs** (AUS) & **P.Hanley** (AUS) ....[7]
34. R.Kendrick (USA) & V.Spadea (USA)
W.Arthurs & P.Hanley [7] ....6/7(1) 6/4 6/4 6/4
35. R.Leach (USA) & B.MacPhie (USA)
36. N.Davydenko (RUS) & J-L.De Jager (RSA)
R.Leach & B.MacPhie 6/2 6/2 6/3
W.Arthurs & P.Hanley [7] ....6/7(11) 6/4 7/5 6/4
(L) 37. S.Draper (AUS) & P.Luczak (AUS)
38. D.Ferrer (ESP) & A.Martin (ESP)
S.Draper & P.Luczak ....4/6 7/5 7/6(5) 6/4
W.Arthurs & P.Hanley [7] ....7/6(7) 5/7 7/6(4) 6/4
39. A.Portas (ESP) & T.Robredo (ESP)
40. **J.Eagle** (AUS) & **J.Palmer** (USA) ....[9]
J.Eagle & J.Palmer [9] 4/6 6/3 6/4 6/4
J.Eagle & J.Palmer [9] ....7/6(2) 6/3 6/4
41. **P.Haarhuis** (NED) & **Y.Kafelnikov** (RUS) ....[14]
(Q) 42. M.Chiudinelli (SUI) & L.Zovko (CRO)
P.Haarhuis & Y.Kafelnikov [14] 6/1 6/2 6/2
J.Bjorkman & T.A.Woodbridge [4] 6/3 6/4 7/5
43. X.Malisse (BEL) & T.Vanhoudt (BEL)
44. F.Lopez (ESP) & F.Vicente (ESP)
X.Malisse & T.Vanhoudt ....6/3 1/1 Ret'd.
P.Haarhuis & Y.Kafelnikov [14] 4/6 7/5 7/5 6/2
45. J.Melzer (AUT) & J.Nieminen (FIN)
46. H.Arazi (MAR) & Y.El Aynaoui (MAR)
H.Arazi & Y.El Aynaoui ....7/5 6/4 7/6(6)
J.Bjorkman & T.A.Woodbridge [4] ....w/o
47. M.Ancic (CRO) & J.Knowle (AUT)
48. **J.Bjorkman** (SWE) & **T.A.Woodbridge** (AUS) ....[4]
J.Bjorkman & T.A.Woodbridge [4] 6/4 6/1 6/2
J.Bjorkman & T.A.Woodbridge [4] ....6/2 6/3 0/0 Ret'd.

49. **M.Llodra** (FRA) & **F.Santoro** (FRA) ....[6]
50. J.Thomas (USA) & D.Vacek (CZE)
M.Llodra & F.Santoro [6] 6/1 6/4 6/4
51. D.Adams (RSA) & J.Gimelstob (USA)
52. A.Dupuis (FRA) & P-H.Mathieu (FRA)
D.Adams & J.Gimelstob ....6/4 6/4 6/7(4) 6/3
M.Llodra & F.Santoro [6] 7/5 5/7 4/6 6/3 6/4
(Q) 53. J.Erlich (ISR) & A.Ram (ISR)
54. N.Healey (AUS) & D.Skoch (CZE)
J.Erlich & A.Ram 4/6 7/5 4/6 6/3 6/4
J.Erlich & A.Ram 6/2 6/1 6/3
55. J.Acasuso (ARG) & A.Schneiter (ARG)
56. **F.Cermak** (CZE) & **L.Friedl** (CZE) ....[12]
F.Cermak & L.Friedl [12] ....6/3 3/6 6/3 7/6(3)
J.Erlich & A.Ram 6/3 6/3
57. **T.Cibulec** (CZE) & **P.Vizner** (CZE) ....[16]
58. D.Hrbaty (SVK) & A.Sa (BRA)
D.Hrbaty & A.Sa 2/6 6/3 6/4
D.Hrbaty & A.Sa 5/7 6/4 6/4 6/4
59. O.Fukarek (CZE) & P.Luxa (CZE)
60. H-T.Lee (KOR) & V.Voltchkov (BLR)
O.Fukarek & P.Luxa 6/4 3/6 1/0
M.Knowles & D.Nestor [2] ....6/3 7/6(5) 7/5
61. S.Humphries (USA) & M.Merklein (BAH)
(W) 62. M.Lee (GBR) & M.MacLagan (GBR)
M.Lee & M.MacLagan ....7/6(2) 7/6(6) 6/4
M.Knowles & D.Nestor [2] 4/6 6/3 6/2 7/5
63. A.Olhovskiy (RUS) & S.Sargsian (ARM)
64. **M.Knowles** (BAH) & **D.Nestor** (CAN) ....[2]
M.Knowles & D.Nestor [2] ....7/6(4) 7/6(4) 7/6(6)

Quarter-Finals

M.Bhupathi & M.Mirnyi [1] ....6/7(6) 6/4 7/6(7) 6/3

L.Paes & D.Rikl [5] ....6/2 6/7(5) 6/2 6/3

J.Bjorkman & T.A.Woodbridge [4] 6/3 6/4 7/5

J.Erlich & A.Ram ....7/6(8) 7/6(2) 7/6(7)

Semi-Finals

M.Bhupathi & M.Mirnyi [1] ....6/7(6) 6/4 7/6(7) 6/3

J.Bjorkman & T.A.Woodbridge [4] 6/2 4/6 6/2 6/1

Final

J.Bjorkman & T.A.Woodbridge [4] ....3/6 6/3 7/6(4) 6/3

THE LADIES' SINGLES CHAMPIONSHIP

Holder: Miss S Williams

The winner becomes the holder, for the year only, of the CHALLENGE TROPHY presented by The All England Lawn Tennis and Croquet Club. The winner receives a silver replica of the Trophy. A silver salver is presented to the runner-up and a bronze medal to each defeated semi-finalist.

First Round

1. **Williams, Serena [1] *(1)***.................(USA)
2. Craybas, Jill *(67)*............................(USA)
3. Callens, Els *(65)*..............................(BEL)
4. Rittner, Barbara *(79)*........................(GER)
5. (Q) Strycova, Barbora *(185)*..................(CZE)
6. Perebiynis, Tatiana *(89)*....................(UKR)
7. Jidkova, Alina *(113)*..........................(RUS)
8. **Granville, Laura [28] *(30)***.............(USA)
9. **Shaughnessy, Meghann [19] *(20)***...(USA)
10. (Q) Kapros, Aniko *(204)*.........................(HUN)
11. Leon Garcia, Gala *(94)*.......................(ESP)
12. (Q) Sucha, Martina *(97)*.........................(SVK)
13. (L) Parra, Arantxa *(111)*.........................(ESP)
14. Ondraskova, Zuzana *(93)*...................(CZE)
15. Roesch, Angelika *(103)*.....................(GER)
16. **Dementieva, Elena [15] *(16)***..........(RUS)
17. **Myskina, Anastasia [10] *(10)***.........(RUS)
18. Nagyova, Henrieta *(82)*.....................(SVK)
19. Krasnoroutskaya, Lina *(44)*...............(RUS)
20. (W) Pullin, Julie *(270)*...........................(GBR)
21. Schett, Barbara *(50)*..........................(AUT)
22. Marrero, Marta *(99)*...........................(ESP)
23. (Q) Sequera, Milagros *(132)*..................(VEN)
24. **Martinez, Conchita [18] *(13)***.........(ESP)
25. **Tanasugarn, Tamarine [32] *(31)***......(THA)
26. Morigami, Akiko *(90)*.........................(JPN)
27. Sprem, Karolina *(71)*.........................(CRO)
28. Benesova, Iveta *(88)*..........................(CZE)
29. Irvin, Marissa *(87)*............................(USA)
30. Mikaelian, Marie-Gaianeh *(38)*.......(SUI)
31. Casanova, Myriam *(53)*.....................(SUI)
32. **Capriati, Jennifer [8] *(7)***...............(USA)
33. **Henin-Hardenne, Justine [3] *(3)***.....(BEL)
34. Vakulenko, Julia *(100)*......................(UKR)
35. (W) Morariu, Corina *(225)*.....................(USA)
36. Pennetta, Flavia *(55)*.........................(ITA)
37. Safina, Dinara *(60)*............................(RUS)
38. Molik, Alicia *(54)*..............................(AUS)
39. Lee-Waters, Lindsay *(105)*.................(USA)
40. **Likhovtseva, Elena [31] *(33)***..........(RUS)
41. **Raymond, Lisa [23] *(24)***..................(USA)
42. Foretz, Stephanie *(84)*.......................(FRA)
43. (W) O'Donoghue, Jane *(260)*..................(GBR)
44. Weingartner, Marlene *(63)*.................(GER)
45. Pierce, Mary *(86)*...............................(FRA)
46. Cargill, Ansley *(92)*............................(USA)
47. Kostanic, Jelena *(123)*.......................(CRO)
48. **Daniilidou, Eleni [14] *(21)***.............(GRE)
49. **Dokic, Jelena [11] *(12)***...................(YUG)
50. (W) Baltacha, Elena *(149)*........................(GBR)
51. Gagliardi, Emmanuelle *(64)*...............(SUI)
52. Cohen Aloro, Stephanie *(78)*..............(FRA)
53. (W) Sharapova, Maria *(91)*......................(RUS)
54. Harkleroad, Ashley *(39)*....................(USA)
55. Obata, Saori *(74)*...............................(JPN)
56. **Bovina, Elena [21] *(22)***...................(RUS)
57. **Stevenson, Alexandra [26] *(28)***.....(USA)
58. Loit, Emilie *(48)*................................(FRA)
59. (Q) Osterloh, Lilia *(226)*..........................(USA)
60. Camerin, Maria Elena *(98)*.................(ITA)
61. Torrens Valero, Cristina *(117)*...........(ESP)
62. Cho, Yoon Jeong *(46)*........................(KOR)
63. (Q) Bielik, Bea *(169)*................................(USA)
64. **Kuznetsova, Svetlana [33] *(34)***......(RUS)
65. **Davenport, Lindsay [5] *(5)***..............(USA)
66. (W) Stosur, Samantha *(147)*....................(AUS)
67. Grande, Rita *(56)*...............................(ITA)
68. Wartusch, Patricia *(96)*......................(AUT)
69. Black, Cara *(59)*................................(ZIM)
70. Kleinova, Sandra *(106)*......................(CZE)
71. Koukalova, Klara *(72)*........................(CZE)
72. **Chladkova, Denisa [30] *(32)***...........(CZE)
73. **Coetzer, Amanda [17] *(15)***..............(RSA)
74. Randriantefy, Dally *(78)*...................(MAD)
75. (L) Noorlander, Seda *(126)*......................(NED)
76. Schiavone, Francesca *(37)*................(ITA)
77. (Q) Lee, Janet *(209)*...............................(TPE)
78. Asagoe, Shinobu *(81)*.........................(JPN)
79. Bartoli, Marion *(52)*...........................(FRA)
80. **Hantuchova, Daniela [9] *(9)***...........(SVK)
81. **Zvonareva, Vera [16] *(17)***..............(RUS)
82. Dominikovic, Evie *(118)*.....................(AUS)
83. Martinez Granados, Conchita *(114)*(ESP)
84. Serra Zanetti, Antonella *(83)*............(ITA)
85. (Q) Gullickson, Carly *(281)*.....................(USA)
86. Tulyaganova, Iroda *(41)*....................(UZB)
87. Mandula, Petra *(57)*..........................(HUN)
88. **Schnyder, Patty [20] *(19)***................(SUI)
89. **Petrova, Nadia [29] *(27)***.................(RUS)
90. Garbin, Tathiana *(102)*......................(ITA)
91. Koulikovskaya, Evgenia *(95)*.............(RUS)
92. Widjaja, Angelique *(70)*.....................(INA)
93. (W) Keothavong, Anne *(145)*....................(GBR)
94. Srebotnik, Katarina *(42)*....................(SLO)
95. (Q) Hrozenska, Stanislava *(194)*............(SVK)
96. **Williams, Venus [4] *(4)***...................(USA)
97. **Rubin, Chanda [7] *(8)***.....................(USA)
98. Majoli, Iva *(68)*.................................(CRO)
99. Talaja, Silvija *(80)*............................(CRO)
100. Frazier, Amy *(51)*...............................(USA)
101. Pratt, Nicole *(76)*...............................(AUS)
102. (Q) Drake, Maureen *(122)*........................(CAN)
103. Sanchez Lorenzo, Maria *(45)*............(ESP)
104. **Farina Elia, Silvia [27] *(25)***............(ITA)
105. **Serna, Magui [24] *(29)***....................(ESP)
106. Ruano Pascual, Virginia *(49)*............(ESP)
107. Pisnik, Tina *(47)*................................(SLO)
108. Matevzic, Maja *(40)*...........................(SLO)
109. Suarez, Paola *(35)*.............................(ARG)
110. (Q) Sfar, Selima *(164)*............................(TUN)
111. Barna, Anca *(61)*................................(GER)
112. **Maleeva, Magdalena [12] *(11)***.........(BUL)
113. **Sugiyama, Ai [13] *(14)***....................(JPN)
114. (W) Ahl, Lucie *(211)*................................(GBR)
115. Cervanova, Ludmila *(85)*...................(SVK)
116. (Q) Fislova, Eva *(131)*.............................(SVK)
117. Bedanova, Daja *(66)*..........................(CZE)
118. Poutchek, Tatiana *(121)*....................(BLR)
119. Husarova, Janette *(73)*......................(SVK)
120. **Dechy, Nathalie [22] *(23)***...............(FRA)
121. **Pistolesi, Anna [25] *(26)***................(ISR)
122. Reeves, Samantha *(109)*....................(USA)
123. Zuluaga, Fabiola *(43)*........................(COL)
124. Fernandez, Clarisa *(62)*....................(ARG)
125. Razzano, Virginie *(58)*.......................(FRA)
126. Rodionova, Anastassia *(116)*.............(RUS)
127. Neffa-De Los Rios, Rossana *(110)*..(PAR)
128. **Clijsters, Kim [2] *(2)***.......................(BEL)

Second Round

- **Miss S.Williams [1] *(1)***............6/3 6/3
- Miss E.S.H.Callens *(65)*...........6/3 7/5
- Miss T.Perebiynis *(89)*.....6/4 5/7 11/9
- **Miss L.Granville [28] *(30)***.......6/1 6/4
- Miss A.Kapros *(204)*...............6/3 6/2
- Miss M.Sucha *(97)*............6/2 4/6 6/1
- Miss A.Parra *(111)*..................7/5 6/2
- **Miss E.Dementieva [15] *(16)***...6/2 6/1
- **Miss A.Myskina [10] *(10)***.........6/4 3/0 Ret'd.
- Miss L.Krasnoroutskaya *(44)*....6/3 6/1
- Miss B.Schett *(50)*...................6/1 6/2
- **Miss C.Martinez [18] *(13)***.5/7 7/5 6/1
- Miss A.Morigami *(90)*.............6/4 6/3
- Miss K.Sprem *(71)*.............6/2 7/6(6)
- Miss M-G.Mikaelian *(38)*..7/5 2/6 8/6
- **Miss J.Capriati [8] *(7)***.............6/1 6/3
- **Mrs J.Henin-Hardenne [3] *(3)***.7/5 6/1
- Miss F.Pennetta *(55)*................6/3 6/2
- Miss A.Molik *(54)*............6/1 4/6 6/4
- **Miss E.Likhovtseva [31] *(33)***.....4/6 6/2 8/6
- **Miss L.M.Raymond [23] *(24)***...6/3 6/3
- Miss M.Weingartner *(63)*........6/4 6/2
- Miss M.Pierce *(86)*..................6/0 6/0
- **Miss E.Daniilidou [14] *(21)***.....6/2 6/2
- **Miss J.Dokic [11] *(12)***.......6/3 1/6 6/4
- Miss E.Gagliardi *(64)*........6/2 4/6 6/3
- Miss M.Sharapova *(91)*...........6/2 6/1
- **Miss E.Bovina [21] *(22)***.7/6(5) 2/6 8/6
- Miss E.Loit *(48)*..................7/5 7/6(2)
- Miss M.Camerin *(98)*..............6/1 6/4
- Miss Y.J.Cho *(46)*..............7/5 1/6 9/7
- **Miss S.Kuznetsova [33] *(34)***....6/1 6/3
- **Miss L.Davenport [5] *(5)***.....7/6(3) 7/5
- Miss R.Grande *(56)*.................6/1 6/4
- Miss C.Black *(59)*....................6/2 6/3
- **Miss D.Chladkova [30] *(32)***.....6/4 6/3
- **Miss A.J.Coetzer [17] *(15)***.6/1 3/6 6/3
- Miss F.Schiavone *(37)*.............6/2 6/2
- Miss S.Asagoe *(81)*.............6/3 7/6(2)
- **Miss D.Hantuchova [9] *(9)***.......6/4 6/1
- **Miss V.Zvonareva [16] *(17)***......6/0 6/2
- Miss C.Martinez Granados *(114)*0/6 6/3 10/8
- Miss I.Tulyaganova *(41)*..........7/5 6/4
- Miss P.Mandula *(57)*...........7/6(2) 6/3
- **Miss N.Petrova [29] *(27)***.........6/1 6/3
- Miss A.Widjaja *(70)*................7/5 6/1
- Miss K.Srebotnik *(42)*....6/2 4/0 Ret'd.
- **Miss V.Williams [4] *(4)***............6/2 6/2
- **Miss C.Rubin [7] *(8)***.................6/3 6/0
- Miss A.Frazier *(51)*.................6/2 6/2
- Miss M.Drake *(122)*..........4/6 6/4 6/4
- **Mrs S.Farina Elia [27] *(25)***.........6/4 6/2
- **Miss M.Serna [24] *(29)***..........6/3 7/5
- Miss M.Matevzic *(40)*...7/6(6) 2/6 6/4
- Miss P.Suarez *(35)*..................6/1 6/2
- **Miss M.Maleeva [12] *(11)***.......6/0 6/1
- **Miss A.Sugiyama [13] *(14)*** 3/6 6/4 6/4
- Miss E.Fislova *(131)*......7/6(2) 2/6 6/4
- Miss D.Bedanova *(66)*.......6/3 4/6 6/4
- **Miss N.Dechy [22] *(23)***...........6/3 6/2
- Miss S.Reeves *(109)*................6/4 6/4
- Miss F.Zuluaga *(43)*.................6/4 6/2
- Miss V.Razzano *(58)*...............6/3 6/1
- **Miss K.Clijsters [2] *(2)***............6/0 6/0

Third Round

- **Miss S.Williams [1] *(1)***......................................6/4 6/4
- **Miss L.Granville [28] *(30)***......................................6/2 6/3
- Miss A.Kapros *(204)*......................................6/0 6/4
- **Miss E.Dementieva [15] *(16)***......................................6/1 6/1
- **Miss A.Myskina [10] *(10)***......................................6/1 6/4
- **Miss C.Martinez [18] *(13)***......................................6/2 6/4
- Miss A.Morigami *(90)*......................................6/3 6/3
- **Miss J.Capriati [8] *(7)***......................................6/2 6/1
- **Mrs J.Henin-Hardenne [3] *(3)***......................................7/6(2) 6/1
- Miss A.Molik *(54)*......................................6/3 6/4
- **Miss L.M.Raymond [23] *(24)***......................................6/3 6/0
- Miss M.Pierce *(86)*......................................6/4 6/1
- **Miss J.Dokic [11] *(12)***......................................6/1 6/3
- Miss M.Sharapova *(91)*......................................6/3 6/1
- Miss E.Loit *(48)*......................................3/6 6/2 6/3
- **Miss S.Kuznetsova [33] *(34)***......................................7/6(2) 6/4
- **Miss L.Davenport [5] *(5)***......................................6/3 6/1
- Miss C.Black *(59)*......................................6/3 7/5
- Miss F.Schiavone *(37)*......................................4/6 7/5 6/4
- Miss S.Asagoe *(81)*......................................0/6 6/4 12/10
- **Miss V.Zvonareva [16] *(17)***......................................6/3 6/1
- Miss I.Tulyaganova *(41)*......................................6/3 6/4
- **Miss N.Petrova [29] *(27)***......................................7/6(3) 6/3
- **Miss V.Williams [4] *(4)***......................................6/4 6/1
- **Miss C.Rubin [7] *(8)***......................................6/4 6/4
- **Mrs S.Farina Elia [27] *(25)***......................................7/6(3) 6/1
- Miss M.Matevzic *(40)*......................................4/6 6/3 6/4
- Miss P.Suarez *(35)*......................................2/6 6/2 6/3
- **Miss A.Sugiyama [13] *(14)***......................................6/1 6/7(6) 7/5
- **Miss N.Dechy [22] *(23)***......................................6/2 6/4
- Miss S.Reeves *(109)*......................................7/6(6) 6/4
- **Miss K.Clijsters [2] *(2)***......................................6/1 6/3

Fourth Round

- **Miss S.Williams [1] *(1)***......................................6/3 6/1
- **Miss E.Dementieva [15] *(16)***......................................6/3 6/1
- **Miss A.Myskina [10] *(10)***......................................6/3 6/3
- **Miss J.Capriati [8] *(7)***......................................6/4 6/4
- **Mrs J.Henin-Hardenne [3] *(3)***......................................6/4 6/4
- Miss M.Pierce *(86)*......................................4/6 6/3 7/5
- Miss M.Sharapova *(91)*......................................6/4 6/4
- **Miss S.Kuznetsova [33] *(34)***......................................6/1 6/2
- **Miss L.Davenport [5] *(5)***......................................6/2 6/2
- Miss S.Asagoe *(81)*......................................7/5 6/2
- **Miss V.Zvonareva [16] *(17)***......................................6/3 7/5
- **Miss V.Williams [4] *(4)***......................................6/1 6/2
- **Mrs S.Farina Elia [27] *(25)***......................................7/6(6) 6/3
- Miss P.Suarez *(35)*......................................5/7 6/3 7/5
- **Miss A.Sugiyama [13] *(14)***......................................6/4 6/4
- **Miss K.Clijsters [2] *(2)***......................................6/1 6/2

Quarter-Finals

- **Miss S.Williams [1] *(1)***......................................6/2 6/2
- **Miss J.Capriati [8] *(7)***......................................6/2 6/3
- **Mrs J.Henin-Hardenne [3] *(3)***......................................6/3 6/3
- **Miss S.Kuznetsova [33] *(34)***......................................6/1 2/6 7/5
- **Miss L.Davenport [5] *(5)***......................................6/4 6/1
- **Miss V.Williams [4] *(4)***......................................6/1 6/3
- **Mrs S.Farina Elia [27] *(25)***......................................7/5 7/6(3)
- **Miss K.Clijsters [2] *(2)***......................................6/3 6/2

Semi-Finals

- **Miss S.Williams [1] *(1)*** 2/6 6/2 6/3
- **Miss J.Henin-Hardenne [3] *(3)*** 6/2 6/2
- **Miss V.Williams [4] *(4)*** 6/2 2/6 6/1
- **Miss K.Clijsters [2] *(2)*** 5/7 6/0 6/1

Final

- **Miss S.Williams [1] *(1)*** 6/3 6/2
- **Miss V.Williams [4] *(4)*** 4/6 6/3 6/1

Miss S.Williams [1] *(1)* 4/6 6/4 6/2

Heavy type denotes seeded players. The figure in brackets against names denotes the order in which they have been seeded. (W) = Wild card. (Q) = Qualifier. (L) = Lucky loser.

The matches are the best of three sets

The winners become the holders, for the year only, of the CHALLENGE CUP presented by HRH PRINCESS MARINA, DUCHESS OF KENT, the late President of The All England Lawn Tennis and Croquet Club. The winners receive silver replicas of the Challenge Cup. A silver salver is presented to each of the runners-up and a bronze medal to each defeated semi-finalist.

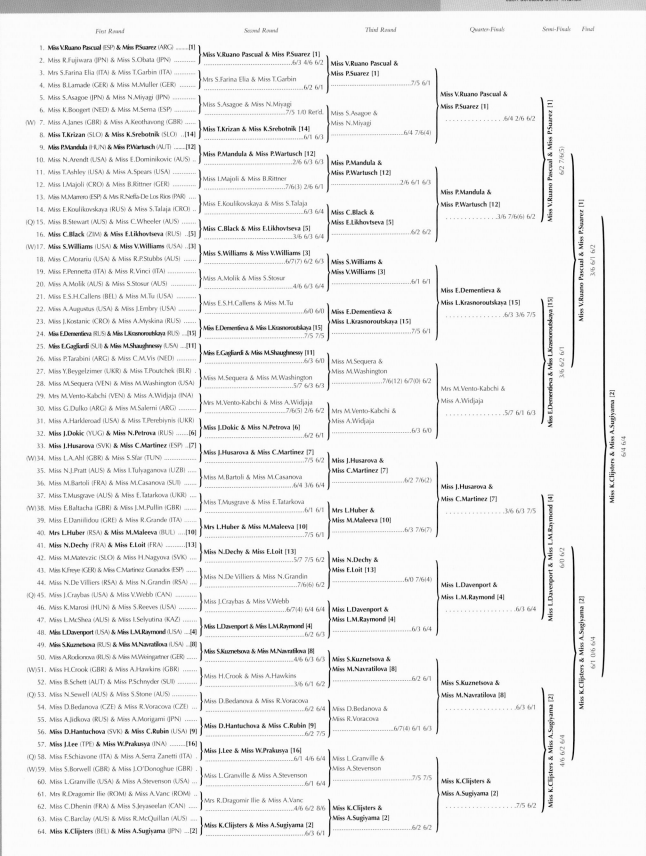

First Round	Second Round	Third Round	Quarter-Finals	Semi-Finals	Final

1. Miss V.Ruano Pascual (ESP) & Miss P.Suarez (ARG) ....[1]
2. Miss R.Fujiwara (JPN) & Miss S.Obata (JPN) ....
3. Mrs S.Farina Elia (ITA) & Miss T.Garbin (ITA) ....
4. Miss B.Lamade (GER) & Miss M.Muller (GER) ....
5. Miss S.Asagoe (JPN) & Miss N.Miyagi (JPN) ....
6. Miss K.Boogert (NED) & Miss M.Serna (ESP) ....
(W) 7. Miss A.Janes (GBR) & Miss A.Keothavong (GBR) ......
8. Miss T.Krizan (SLO) & Miss K.Srebotnik (SLO) ..[14]
9. Miss P.Mandula (HUN) & Miss P.Wartusch (AUT) ....[12]
10. Miss N.Arendt (USA) & E.Dominikovic (AUS) ..
11. Miss T.Ashley (USA) & Miss A.Spears (USA) ....
12. Miss I.Majoli (CRO) & Miss B.Rittner (GER) ....
13. Miss M.Marrero (ESP) & Mrs R.Neffa-De Los Rios (PAR) ....
14. Miss E.Koulikovskaya (RUS) & Miss S.Talaja (CRO) ..
(Q) 15. Miss B.Stewart (AUS) & Miss C.Wheeler (AUS) ....
16. Miss C.Black (ZIM) & Miss E.Likhovtseva (RUS) ..[5]
(W)17. Miss S.Williams (USA) & Miss V.Williams (USA) ..[3]
18. Miss C.Morariu (USA) & Miss R.P.Stubbs (AUS) ......
19. Miss F.Pennetta (ITA) & Miss R.Vinci (ITA) ....
20. Miss A.Molik (AUS) & Miss S.Stosur (AUS) ....
21. Miss E.S.H.Callens (BEL) & Miss M.Tu (USA) ....
22. Miss A.Augustus (USA) & Miss J.Embry (USA) ....
23. Miss J.Kostanic (CRO) & Miss A.Myskina (RUS) ....
24. Miss E.Dementieva (RUS) & Miss L.Krasnoroutskaya (RUS) ....[15]
25. Miss E.Gagliardi (SUI) & Miss M.Shaughnessy (USA) ...[11]
26. Miss P.Tarabini (ARG) & Miss C.M.Vis (NED) ....
27. Miss Y.Beygelzimer (UKR) & Miss T.Poutchek (BLR) .
28. Miss M.Sequera (VEN) & Miss M.Washington (USA) ...
29. Miss M.Vento-Kabchi (VEN) & Miss A.Widjaja (INA) ...
30. Miss G.Dulko (ARG) & Miss M.Salerni (ARG) ....
31. Miss A.Harkleroad (USA) & Miss T.Perebiynis (UKR) ...
32. Miss J.Dokic (YUG) & Miss N.Petrova (RUS) ....[6]
33. Miss J.Husarova (SVK) & Miss C.Martinez (ESP) ..[7]
(W)34. Miss L.A.Ahl (GBR) & Miss S.Sfar (TUN) ....
35. Miss N.J.Pratt (AUS) & Miss I.Tulyaganova (UZB) .....
36. Miss M.Bartoli (FRA) & Miss M.Casanova (SUI) .....
37. Miss T.Musgrave (AUS) & Miss E.Tatarkova (UKR) ....
(W)38. Miss E.Baltacha (GBR) & Miss J.M.Pullin (GBR) .....
39. Miss E.Daniilidou (GRE) & Miss R.Grande (ITA) ......
40. Mrs L.Huber (RSA) & Miss M.Maleeva (BUL) ....[10]
41. Miss N.Dechy (FRA) & Miss E.Loit (FRA) ....[13]
42. Miss M.Matevzic (SLO) & Miss H.Nagyova (SVK) .....
43. Miss K.Freye (GER) & Miss C.Martinez Granados (ESP) ......
44. Miss N.De Villiers (RSA) & Miss N.Grandin (RSA) ....
(Q) 45. Miss J.Craybas (USA) & Miss V.Webb (CAN) ....
46. Miss K.Marosi (HUN) & Miss S.Reeves (USA) ....
47. Miss L.McShea (AUS) & Miss M.Selyutina (KAZ) .....
48. Miss L.Davenport (USA) & Miss L.M.Raymond (USA) ..[4]
49. Miss S.Kuznetsova (RUS) & Miss M.Navratilova (USA) ..[8]
50. Miss A.Rodionova (RUS) & Miss M.Weingartner (GER) ..
(W)51. Miss H.Crook (GBR) & Miss A.Hawkins (GBR) .....
52. Miss B.Schett (AUT) & Miss P.Schnyder (SUI) ......
(Q) 53. Miss N.Sewell (AUS) & Miss S.Stone (AUS) ....
54. Miss D.Bedanova (CZE) & Miss R.Voracova (CZE) ...
55. Miss A.Jidkova (RUS) & Miss A.Morigami (JPN) .....
56. Miss D.Hantuchova (SVK) & Miss C.Rubin (USA) [9]
57. Miss J.Lee (TPE) & Miss W.Prakusya (INA) ....[16]
(Q) 58. Miss F.Schiavone (ITA) & Miss A.Serra Zanetti (ITA) ..
(W)59. Miss S.Borwell (GBR) & Miss J.O'Donoghue (GBR) ..
60. Miss L.Granville (USA) & Miss A.Stevenson (USA) ....
61. Mrs R.Dragomir Ilie (ROM) & Miss A.Vanc (ROM) ....
62. Miss C.Dhenin (FRA) & Miss S.Jeyaseelan (CAN) ....
63. Miss C.Barclay (AUS) & Miss R.McQuillan (AUS) ....
64. Miss K.Clijsters (BEL) & Miss A.Sugiyama (JPN) ...[2]

Second Round

Miss V.Ruano Pascual & Miss P.Suarez [1] 6/3 4/6 6/2

Mrs S.Farina Elia & Miss T.Garbin 6/2 6/1

Miss S.Asagoe & Miss N.Miyagi ....7/5 1/0 Ret'd.

Miss T.Krizan & Miss K.Srebotnik [14] 6/1 6/3

Miss P.Mandula & Miss P.Wartusch [12] 2/6 6/3 6/3

Miss I.Majoli & Miss B.Rittner ....7/6(3) 2/6 6/1

Miss E.Koulikovskaya & Miss S.Talaja 6/4

Miss C.Black & Miss E.Likhovtseva [5] 3/6 6/3 6/4

Miss S.Williams & Miss V.Williams [3] ....6/7(7) 6/2 6/3

Miss A.Molik & Miss S.Stosur 4/6 6/3 6/4

Miss E.S.H.Callens & Miss M.Tu 6/0 6/0

Miss E.Dementieva & Miss L.Krasnoroutskaya [15] 7/5 7/5

Miss E.Gagliardi & Miss M.Shaughnessy [11] 6/3 6/0

Miss M.Sequera & Miss M.Washington 5/7 6/3 6/3

Mrs M.Vento-Kabchi & Miss A.Widjaja ....7/6(5) 2/6 6/2

Miss J.Dokic & Miss N.Petrova [6] 6/2 6/1

Miss J.Husarova & Miss C.Martinez [7] 7/5 6/2

Miss M.Bartoli & Miss M.Casanova 6/4 3/6 6/4

Miss T.Musgrave & Miss E.Tatarkova 6/1 6/3

Mrs L.Huber & Miss M.Maleeva [10] 7/5 6/1

Miss N.Dechy & Miss E.Loit [13] 5/7 7/5 6/2

Miss N.De Villiers & Miss N.Grandin ....7/6(6) 6/2

Miss J.Craybas & Miss V.Webb ....6/7(4) 6/4 6/4

Miss L.Davenport & Miss L.M.Raymond [4] 6/2 6/3

Miss S.Kuznetsova & Miss M.Navratilova [8] 4/6 6/3 6/3

Miss H.Crook & Miss A.Hawkins 3/6 6/1 6/2

Miss D.Bedanova & Miss R.Voracova 6/2 6/4

Miss D.Hantuchova & Miss C.Rubin [9] 6/2 7/5

Miss J.Lee & Miss W.Prakusya [16] 6/1 4/6 6/4

Miss L.Granville & Miss A.Stevenson 6/1 6/4

Mrs R.Dragomir Ilie & Miss A.Vanc 4/6 6/2 8/6

Miss K.Clijsters & Miss A.Sugiyama [2] 6/3 6/1

Third Round

Miss V.Ruano Pascual & Miss P.Suarez [1] 7/5 6/1

Miss S.Asagoe & Miss N.Miyagi ....6/4 7/6(4)

Miss P.Mandula & Miss P.Wartusch [12] 2/6 6/1 6/3

Miss C.Black & Miss E.Likhovtseva [5] 6/2 6/2

Miss S.Williams & Miss V.Williams [3] 6/1 6/1

Miss E.Dementieva & Miss L.Krasnoroutskaya [15] 7/5 6/1

Miss M.Sequera & Miss M.Washington ....7/6(12) 6/7(0) 6/2

Mrs M.Vento-Kabchi & Miss A.Widjaja 6/3 6/0

Miss J.Husarova & Miss C.Martinez [7] ....6/2 7/6(2)

Mrs L.Huber & Miss M.Maleeva [10] ....6/3 7/6(7)

Miss N.Dechy & Miss E.Loit [13] ....6/0 7/6(4)

Miss L.Davenport & Miss L.M.Raymond [4] 6/3 6/4

Miss S.Kuznetsova & Miss M.Navratilova [8] 6/2 6/1

Miss D.Bedanova & Miss R.Voracova ....6/7(4) 6/1 6/3

Miss L.Granville & Miss A.Stevenson 7/5 7/5

Miss K.Clijsters & Miss A.Sugiyama [2] 6/2 6/2

Quarter-Finals

Miss V.Ruano Pascual & Miss P.Suarez [1] 6/4 2/6 6/2

Miss P.Mandula & Miss P.Wartusch [12] ....3/6 7/6(6) 6/2

Miss E.Dementieva & Miss L.Krasnoroutskaya [15] 6/3 3/6 7/5

Mrs M.Vento-Kabchi & Miss A.Widjaja 5/7 6/1 6/3

Miss J.Husarova & Miss C.Martinez [7] 3/6 6/3 7/5

Miss L.Davenport & Miss L.M.Raymond [4] 6/3 6/4

Miss S.Kuznetsova & Miss M.Navratilova [8] 6/3 6/1

Miss K.Clijsters & Miss A.Sugiyama [2] 7/5 6/2

Semi-Finals

Miss V.Ruano Pascual & Miss P.Suarez [1] ....6/2 7/6(5)

Miss E.Dementieva & Miss L.Krasnoroutskaya [15] 3/6 6/2 6/1

Miss J.Husarova & Miss C.Martinez [7] 6/0 6/2

Miss K.Clijsters & Miss A.Sugiyama [2] 6/1 0/6 6/4

Final

Miss V.Ruano Pascual & Miss P.Suarez [1] 3/6 6/1 6/2

Miss K.Clijsters & Miss A.Sugiyama [2] 4/6 6/2 6/4

Miss V.Ruano Pascual & Miss P.Suarez [1] 6/4 6/4

151

Heavy type denotes seeded players. The figure in brackets against names denotes the order in which they have been seeded. (W) = Wild card. (Q) = Qualifier. (L) = Lucky loser.

The matches are the best of three sets

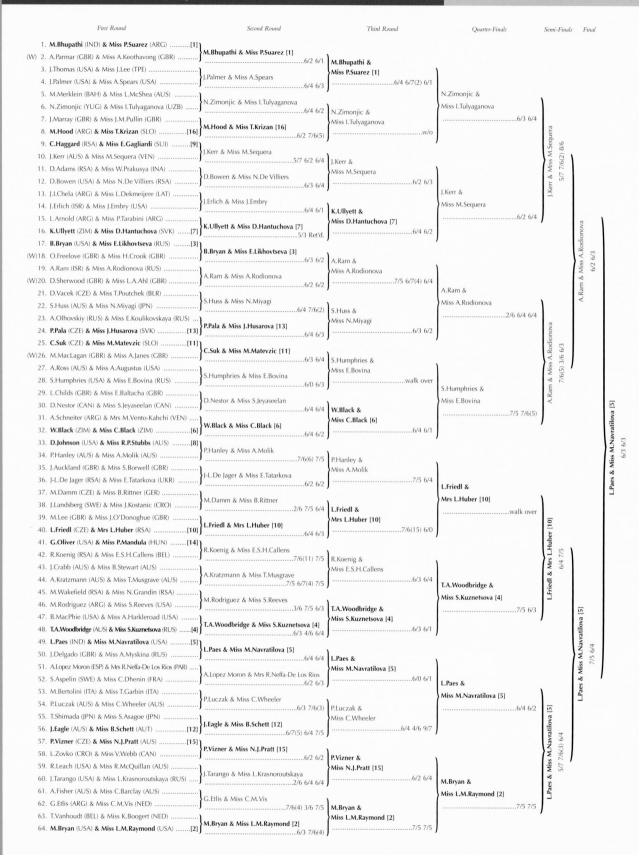

First Round	Second Round	Third Round	Quarter-Finals	Semi-Finals	Final

1. **M.Bhupathi** (IND) & **Miss P.Suarez** (ARG) ....[1]
(W) 2. A.Parmar (GBR) & Miss A.Keothavong (GBR) ....
3. J.Thomas (USA) & Miss J.Lee (TPE) ....
4. J.Palmer (USA) & Miss A.Spears (USA) ....
5. M.Merklein (BAH) & Miss M.McShea (AUS) ....
6. N.Zimonjic (YUG) & Miss I.Tulyaganova (UZB) ....
7. J.Marray (GBR) & Miss J.M.Pullin (GBR) ....
8. **M.Hood** (ARG) & **Miss T.Krizan** (SLO) ....[16]
9. **C.Haggard** (RSA) & **Miss E.Gagliardi** (SUI) ....[9]
10. J.Kerr (AUS) & Miss M.Sequera (VEN) ....
11. D.Adams (RSA) & Miss W.Prakusya (INA) ....
12. D.Bowen (USA) & Miss N.De Villiers (RSA) ....
13. J.I.Chela (ARG) & Miss L.Dekmeijere (LAT) ....
14. J.Erlich (ISR) & Miss J.Embry ....
15. L.Arnold (ARG) & Miss P.Tarabini (ARG) ....
16. **K.Ullyett** (ZIM) & **Miss D.Hantuchova** (SVK) ....[7]
17. **B.Bryan** (USA) & **Miss E.Likhovtseva** (RUS) ....[3]
(W)18. O.Freelove (GBR) & Miss H.Crook (GBR) ....
19. A.Ram (ISR) & Miss A.Rodionova (RUS) ....
(W)20. D.Sherwood (GBR) & Miss L.A.Ahl (GBR) ....
21. D.Vacek (CZE) & Miss T.Poutchek (BLR) ....
22. S.Huss (AUS) & Miss N.Miyagi (JPN) ....
23. A.Olhovskiy (RUS) & Miss E.Koulikovskaya (RUS) ...
24. **P.Pala** (CZE) & **Miss J.Husarova** (SVK) ....[13]
25. **C.Suk** (CZE) & **Miss M.Matevzic** (SLO) ....[11]
(W)26. M.MacLagan (GBR) & Miss A.Janes (GBR) ....
27. A.Ross (AUS) & Miss A.Augustus (USA) ....
28. S.Humphries (USA) & Miss E.Bovina (RUS) ....
29. L.Childs (GBR) & Miss E.Baltacha (GBR) ....
30. D.Nestor (CAN) & Miss S.Jeyaseelan (CAN) ....
31. A.Schneiter (ARG) & Mrs M.Vento-Kabchi (VEN) ....
32. **W.Black** (ZIM) & **Miss C.Black** (ZIM) ....[6]
33. **D.Johnson** (USA) & **Miss R.P.Stubbs** (AUS) ....[8]
34. P.Hanley (AUS) & Miss A.Molik (AUS) ....
35. J.Auckland (GBR) & Miss S.Borwell (GBR) ....
36. J-L.De Jager (RSA) & Miss E.Tatarkova (UKR) ....
37. M.Damm (CZE) & Miss B.Rittner (GER) ....
38. J.Landsberg (SWE) & Miss J.Kostanic (CRO) ....
39. M.Lee (GBR) & Miss J.O'Donoghue (GBR) ....
40. **L.Friedl** (CZE) & **Mrs L.Huber** (RSA) ....[10]
41. **G.Oliver** (USA) & **Miss P.Mandula** (HUN) ....[14]
42. R.Koenig (RSA) & Miss E.S.H.Callens (BEL) ....
43. J.Crabb (AUS) & Miss B.Stewart (AUS) ....
44. A.Kratzmann (AUS) & Miss T.Musgrave (AUS) ....
45. M.Wakefield (RSA) & Miss N.Grandin (RSA) ....
46. M.Rodriguez (ARG) & Miss S.Reeves (USA) ....
47. B.MacPhie (USA) & Miss A.Harkleroad (USA) ....
48. **T.A.Woodbridge** (AUS) & **Miss S.Kuznetsova** (RUS) ....[4]
49. **L.Paes** (IND) & **Miss M.Navratilova** (USA) ....[5]
50. J.Delgado (GBR) & Miss A.Myskina (RUS) ....
51. A.Lopez Moron (ESP) & Miss R.Neffa-De Los Rios (PAR) ...
52. S.Aspelin (SWE) & Miss C.Dhenin (FRA) ....
53. M.Bertolini (ITA) & Miss T.Garbin (ITA) ....
54. P.Luczak (AUS) & Miss C.Wheeler (AUS) ....
55. T.Shimada (JPN) & Miss S.Asagoe (JPN) ....
56. **J.Eagle** (AUS) & **Miss B.Schett** (AUT) ....[12]
57. **P.Vizner** (CZE) & **Miss N.J.Pratt** (AUS) ....[15]
58. L.Zovko (CRO) & Miss V.Webb (CAN) ....
59. R.Leach (USA) & Miss R.McQuillan (AUS) ....
60. J.Tarango (USA) & Miss L.Krasnoroutskaya (RUS) ....
61. A.Fisher (AUS) & Miss C.Barclay (AUS) ....
62. G.Etlis (ARG) & Miss C.M.Vis (NED) ....
63. T.Vanhoudt (BEL) & Miss K.Boogert (NED) ....
64. **M.Bryan** (USA) & **Miss L.M.Raymond** (USA) ....[2]

Second Round

M.Bhupathi & Miss P.Suarez [1] — 6/2 6/1
J.Palmer & Miss A.Spears — 6/4 6/3
N.Zimonjic & Miss I.Tulyaganova — 6/4 6/2
M.Hood & Miss T.Krizan [16] — 6/2 7/6(5)
J.Kerr & Miss M.Sequera — 5/7 6/2 6/4
D.Bowen & Miss N.De Villiers — 6/3 6/4
J.Erlich & Miss J.Embry — 6/4 6/1
K.Ullyett & Miss D.Hantuchova [7] — 5/3 Ret'd.
B.Bryan & Miss E.Likhovtseva [3] — 6/3 6/2
A.Ram & Miss A.Rodionova — 6/2 6/2
S.Huss & Miss N.Miyagi — 6/4 7/6(2)
P.Pala & Miss J.Husarova [13] — 6/4 6/3
C.Suk & Miss M.Matevzic [11] — 6/3 6/4
S.Humphries & Miss E.Bovina — 6/0 6/3
D.Nestor & Miss S.Jeyaseelan — 6/4 6/4
W.Black & Miss C.Black [6] — 6/4 6/2
P.Hanley & Miss A.Molik — 7/6(6) 7/5
J-L.De Jager & Miss E.Tatarkova — 6/2 6/2
M.Damm & Miss B.Rittner — 2/6 7/5 6/4
L.Friedl & Mrs L.Huber [10] — 6/4 6/3
R.Koenig & Miss E.S.H.Callens — 7/6(11) 7/5
A.Kratzmann & Miss T.Musgrave — 7/5 6/7(4) 7/5
M.Rodriguez & Miss S.Reeves — 3/6 7/5 6/3
T.A.Woodbridge & Miss S.Kuznetsova [4] — 6/3 4/6 6/4
L.Paes & Miss M.Navratilova [5] — 6/4 6/3
A.Lopez Moron & Mrs R.Neffa-De Los Rios — 6/2 6/3
P.Luczak & Miss C.Wheeler — 6/3 7/6(3)
J.Eagle & Miss B.Schett [12] — 6/7(5) 6/4 7/5
P.Vizner & Miss N.J.Pratt [15] — 6/2 6/2
J.Tarango & Miss L.Krasnoroutskaya — 2/6 6/4 6/4
G.Etlis & Miss C.M.Vis — 7/6(4) 3/6 7/5
M.Bryan & Miss L.M.Raymond [2] — 6/3 7/6(4)

Third Round

M.Bhupathi & Miss P.Suarez [1] — 6/4 6/7(2) 6/1
N.Zimonjic & Miss I.Tulyaganova — w/o
J.Kerr & Miss M.Sequera — 6/2 6/3
K.Ullyett & Miss D.Hantuchova [7] — 6/4 6/2
A.Ram & Miss A.Rodionova — 7/5 6/7(4) 6/4
S.Huss & Miss N.Miyagi — 6/3 6/2
S.Humphries & Miss E.Bovina — walk over
W.Black & Miss C.Black [6] — 6/4 6/1
P.Hanley & Miss A.Molik — 7/5 6/4
L.Friedl & Mrs L.Huber [10] — 7/6(15) 6/0
R.Koenig & Miss E.S.H.Callens — 6/3 6/4
T.A.Woodbridge & Miss S.Kuznetsova [4] — 6/3 6/1
L.Paes & Miss M.Navratilova [5] — 6/0 6/1
P.Luczak & Miss C.Wheeler — 6/4 4/6 9/7
P.Vizner & Miss N.J.Pratt [15] — 6/2 6/4
M.Bryan & Miss L.M.Raymond [2] — 7/5 7/5

Quarter-Finals

N.Zimonjic & Miss I.Tulyaganova — 6/3 6/4
J.Kerr & Miss M.Sequera — 6/2 6/4
A.Ram & Miss A.Rodionova — 2/6 6/4 6/4
S.Humphries & Miss E.Bovina — 7/5 7/6(5)
L.Friedl & Mrs L.Huber [10] — walk over
T.A.Woodbridge & Miss S.Kuznetsova [4] — 7/5 6/3
L.Paes & Miss M.Navratilova [5] — 6/4 6/2
M.Bryan & Miss L.M.Raymond [2] — 7/5 7/5

Semi-Finals

J.Kerr & Miss M.Sequera — 5/7 7/6(2) 8/6
A.Ram & Miss A.Rodionova — 7/6(5) 3/6 6/3
L.Friedl & Mrs L.Huber [10] — 6/4 7/5
L.Paes & Miss M.Navratilova [5] — 5/7 7/6(3) 6/4

Final

A.Ram & Miss A.Rodionova — 6/2 6/3
L.Paes & Miss M.Navratilova [5] — 6/3 6/3

THE 35 AND OVER GENTLEMEN'S INVITATION DOUBLES

Holders: S Davis and D Pate

GROUP A

	S. Davis (USA) and D. Pate (USA)	G.W. Donnelly (USA) and L. Jensen (USA)	H. Guenthardt (SUI) and B. Taroczy (HUN)	J. Nystrom (SWE) and M. Pernfors (SWE)	WINS	LOSSES
S. Davis (USA) and D. Pate (USA)		4/6 6/2 2/6 L	6/2 6/0 W	6/1 6/7(3) 6/2 W	2	1
G.W. Donnelly (USA) and L. Jensen (USA)	6/4 2/6 6/2 W		6/4 6/7(5) 6/3 W	7/6(2) 6/4 W	3	0
H. Guenthardt (SUI) and B. Taroczy (HUN)	2/6 0/6 L	4/6 7/6(5) 3/6 L		6/7(3) 4/6 L	0	3
J. Nystrom (SWE) and M. Pernfors (SWE)	1/6 7/6(3) 2/6 L	6/7(2) 4/6 L	7/6(3) 6/4 W		1	2

Semi-final: G.W. Donnelly (USA) and L. Jensen (USA)

GROUP B

	N. Broad (GBR) and P. Hand (GBR)	S. Casal (ESP) and E. Sanchez (ESP)	K Flach (USA) and R. Seguso (USA)	T-J Middleton (USA) and S. Zivojinovic (YUG)	WINS	LOSSES
N. Broad (GBR) and P. Hand (GBR)		1/6 2/6 L	3/6 6/3 7/5 W	7/6(5) 7/6(6) W	2	1
S. Casal (ESP) and E. Sanchez (ESP)	6/1 6/2 W		1/6 4/6 L	7/5 6/2 W	2	1
K Flach (USA) and R. Seguso (USA)	6/3 3/6 5/7 L	6/1 6/4 W		6/4 6/2 W	2	1
T-J Middleton (USA) and S. Zivojinovic (YUG)	6/7(5) 6/7(6) L	5/7 2/6 L	4/6 2/6 L		0	3

Semi-final: K Flach (USA) and R. Seguso (USA)

GROUP C

	J.B. Fitzgerald (AUS) and M. Kratzmann (AUS)	P. Galbraith (USA) and S. Melville (USA)	J. Grabb (USA) and J. Hlasek (SUI)	D. Rostagno (USA) and L Shiras (USA)	WINS	LOSSES
J.B. Fitzgerald (AUS) and M. Kratzmann (AUS)		2/6 6/3 1/6 L	w/o W	4/6 4/6 L	1	2
P. Galbraith (USA) and S. Melville (USA)	6/2 3/6 6/1 W		w/o W	2/6 6/7(10) L	2	1
J. Grabb (USA) and J. Hlasek (SUI)	w/o L	w/o L		3/6 6/1 3/6 L	0	3
D. Rostagno (USA) and L Shiras (USA)	6/4 6/4 W	6/2 7/6(2) W	6/3 1/6 6/3 W		3	0

Semi-final: D. Rostagno (USA) and L Shiras (USA)

GROUP D

	M.J. Bates (GBR) and N.A. Fulwood (GBR)	P. Aldrich (RSA) and D.Visser (RSA)	J. Frana (ARG) and L. Lavalle (MEX)	A Jarryd (SWE) and H. Leconte (FRA)	WINS	LOSSES
M.J. Bates (GBR) and N.A. Fulwood (GBR)		6/7(6) 7/6(7) 6/4 W	6/0 6/0 W	6/2 7/5 W	3	0
P. Aldrich (RSA) and D.Visser (RSA)	7/6(6) 6/7(7) 4/6 L		1/6 6/2 4/6 L	7/6(4) 5/7 2/6 L	0	3
J. Frana (ARG) and L. Lavalle (MEX)	0/6 0/6 L	6/1 2/6 6/... W		6/7(6) 4/6 L	1	2
A Jarryd (SWE) and H. Leconte (FRA)	2/6 5/7 L	6/7(4) 7/5 6/2 W	7/6(6) 6/4 W		2	1

Semi-final: M.J. Bates (GBR) and N.A. Fulwood (GBR)

SEMI-FINALS / FINAL

- G.W. Donnelly (USA) and L. Jensen (USA) — 6/4 4/6 6/4
- M.J. Bates (GBR) and N.A. Fulwood (GBR) — 6/3 6/1

Winners: M.J. Bates (GBR) and N.A. Fulwood (GBR) 6/2 6/4

This event is played on a 'round robin' basis. Sixteen invited pairs are divided into four groups and each pair in each group plays the others. The pairs winning most matches are the winners of their respective groups and play semi-final and final rounds as indicated above. If matches should be equal in any group, the head-to-head result between the two pairs with the same number of wins determines the winning pair of the group. Heavy type denotes seeded players. **The matches are the best of three sets.** The tie-break will operate at six games all in the first two sets.

THE 45 AND OVER GENTLEMEN'S INVITATION DOUBLES

Holders: C Dowdeswell and C J Mottram

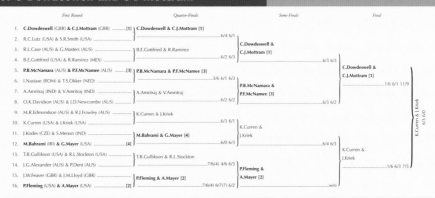

First Round

1. C.Dowdeswell (GBR) & C.J.Mottram (GBR) .... [1]
2. R.C.Lutz (USA) & S.R.Smith (USA)
3. R.L.Case (AUS) & G.Masters (AUS)
4. B.E.Gottfried (USA) & R.Ramirez (MEX)
5. P.B.McNamara (AUS) & P.F.McNamee (AUS) .... [3]
6. I.Nastase (ROM) & T.S.Okker (NED)
7. A.Amritraj (IND) & V.Amritraj (IND)
8. O.K.Davidson (AUS) & J.D.Newcombe (AUS)
9. M.R.Edmondson (AUS) & R.J.Frawley (AUS)
10. K.Curren (USA) & J.Kriek (USA)
11. J.Kodes (CZE) & S.Menon (IND)
12. M.Bahrami (IRI) & G.Mayer (USA) .... [4]
13. T.R.Gulikson (USA) & R.L.Stockton (USA)
14. J.G.Alexander (AUS) & P.Dent (AUS)
15. J.W.Feaver (GBR) & J.M.Lloyd (GBR)
16. P.Fleming (USA) & A.Mayer (USA) .... [2]

Quarter-Finals

- C.Dowdeswell & C.J.Mottram [1] — 6/4 6/1
- B.E.Gottfried & R.Ramirez — 6/2 6/0
- P.B.McNamara & P.F.McNamee [3] — 3/6 6/1 6/3
- A.Amritraj & V.Amritraj — 6/2 6/2
- K.Curren & J.Kriek — 6/3 6/1
- M.Bahrami & G.Mayer [4] — 6/0 6/3
- T.R.Gulikson & R.L.Stockton — 7/6(4) 4/6 6/3
- P.Fleming & A.Mayer [2] — 7/6(4) 6/7(2) 6/2

Semi-Finals

- C.Dowdeswell & C.J.Mottram [1] — 6/3 6/2
- P.B.McNamara & P.F.McNamee [3] — 6/3 6/2
- K.Curren & J.Kriek — 6/4 6/2
- P.Fleming & A.Mayer [2] — w/o

Final

- C.Dowdeswell & C.J.Mottram [1] — 1/6 6/1 11/9
- K.Curren & J.Kriek — 1/6 6/3 7/5

Winners: K.Curren & J.Kriek 6/3 6/0

Heavy type denotes seeded players. The figure in brackets against names denotes the order in which they have been seeded.
The matches are the best of three sets. The tie-break will operate at six games all in the first two sets.

THE 35 AND OVER LADIES' INVITATION DOUBLES

Holders: Miss M Jausovec and Mrs G Magers

	Miss M. Jausovec (SLO) and Miss H. Sukova (CZE)		Miss R. Casals (USA) and Miss H. Mandlikova (AUS)		Mrs C. Bassett-Seguso (USA) and Miss A. Smith (USA)		Miss J.M. Durie (GBR) and Mrs G. Magers (USA)		WINS	LOSSES	FINAL
GROUP A											
Miss M. Jausovec (SLO) and Miss H. Sukova (CZE)			6/2 6/1	W	6/1 7/5	W	7/5 3/6 5/7	L	2	1	
Miss R. Casals (USA) and Miss H. Mandlikova (AUS)	2/6 1/6	L			1/6 1/6	L	2/6 4/6	L	0	3	
Mrs C. Bassett-Seguso (USA) and Miss A. Smith (USA)	1/6 5/7	L	6/1 6/1	W			2/6 5/7	L	1	2	
Miss J.M. Durie (GBR) and Mrs G. Magers (USA)	5/7 6/3 7/5	W	6/2 6/4	W	6/2 7/5	W			3	0	

	Miss N. Tauziat (FRA) and Miss Y. Vermaak (RSA)		Miss I. Kloss (RSA) and Mrs K. Rinaldi (USA)		Mrs L. Neiland (RUS) and Miss W.M. Turnbull (AUS)		Miss C. Lindqvist (SWE) and Mrs R.D. Nideffer (RSA)		WINS	LOSSES	
GROUP B											
Miss N. Tauziat (FRA) and Miss Y. Vermaak (RSA)			6/3 1/6 4/6	L	6/4 6/4	W	1/6 5/7	L	1	2	
Miss I. Kloss (RSA) and Mrs K. Rinaldi (USA)	3/6 6/1 6/4	W			3/6 7/5 11/9	W	7/6(5) 6/4	W	3	0	
Mrs L. Neiland (RUS) and Miss W.M. Turnbull (AUS)	4/6 4/6	L	6/3 5/7 9/11	L			2/6 5/7	L	0	3	
Miss C. Lindqvist (SWE) and Mrs R.D. Nideffer (RSA)	6/1 7/5	W	6/7(5) 4/6	L	6/2 7/5	W			2	1	

FINAL: Miss J.M. Durie (GBR) and Mrs G. Magers (USA) / Miss I. Kloss (RSA) and Mrs K. Rinaldi (USA) — Winner: Miss I. Kloss (RSA) and Mrs K. Rinaldi (USA) 6/4 4/6 7/5

This event is played on a 'round robin' basis. Eight invited pairs are divided into two groups and each pair in each group plays the others. The pairs winning most matches are the winners of their respective groups and play a final round as indicated above. If matches should be equal in any group, the head-to-head result between the two pairs with the same number of wins determines the winning pair of the group.

Heavy type denotes seeded players.

The matches are the best of three sets.   The tie-break will operate at six games all in the first two sets.

ALPHABETICAL LIST – 35 & OVER EVENTS

GENTLEMEN

Aldrich P. *(South Africa)*
Bates M.J. *(Great Britain)*
Broad N. *(Great Britain)*
Casal S. *(Spain)*
Davis S. *(USA)*
Donnelly G.W. *(USA)*
Fitzgerald J.B. *(Australia)*
Flach K. *(USA)*

Frana J. *(Argentina)*
Fulwood N.A. *(Great Britain)*
Galbraith P. *(USA)*
Grabb J. *(USA)*
Guenthardt H. *(Switzerland)*
Hand P. *(Great Britain)*
Hlasek J. *(Switzerland)*
Jarryd A. *(Sweden)*

Jensen L. *(USA)*
Kratzmann M. *(Australia)*
Lavalle L. *(Mexico)*
Leconte H. *(France)*
Melville S. *(USA)*
Middleton T-J. *(USA)*
Nystrom J. *(Sweden)*
Pate D. *(USA)*

Pernfors M. *(Sweden)*
Rostagno D. *(USA)*
Sanchez E. *(Spain)*
Seguso R. *(USA)*
Shiras L *(USA)*
Taroczy B. *(Hungary)*
Visser D. *(South Africa)*
Zivojinovic S. *(Yugoslavia)*

LADIES

Bassett-Seguso Mrs C. *(USA)*
Casals Miss R. *(USA)*
Durie Miss J.M. *(Great Britain)*
Jausovec Miss M. *(Slovenia)*

Kloss Miss I. *(South Africa)*
Lindqvist Miss C. *(Sweden)*
Magers Mrs G. *(USA)*
Mandlikova Miss H. *(Australia)*

Neiland Mrs L. *(Russia)*
Nideffer Mrs R.D. *(South Africa)*
Rinaldi Mrs K. *(USA)*
Smith Miss A. *(USA)*

Sukova Miss H. *(Czech Republic)*
Tauziat Miss N. *(France)*
Turnbull Miss W.M. *(Australia)*
Vermaak Miss Y. *(South Africa)*

ALPHABETICAL LIST – 45 & OVER EVENT

GENTLEMEN

Alexander J.G. *(Australia)*
Amritraj A. *(India)*
Amritraj V. *(India)*
Bahrami M. *(Iran)*
Case R.L. *(Australia)*
Curren K. *(USA)*
Davidson O.K. *(Australia)*
Dent P. *(Australia)*

Dowdeswell C. *(Great Britain)*
Edmondson M.R. *(Australia)*
Feaver J.W. *(Great Britain)*
Fleming P. *(USA)*
Frawley R.J. *(Australia)*
Gottfried B.E. *(USA)*
Gullikson T.R. *(USA)*
Kodes J. *(Czech Republic)*

Kriek J. *(USA)*
Lloyd J.M. *(Great Britain)*
Lutz R.C. *(USA)*
Masters G. *(Australia)*
Mayer A. *(USA)*
Mayer G. *(USA)*
McNamara P.B. *(Australia)*
McNamee P.F. *(Australia)*

Menon S. *(India)*
Mottram C.J. *(Great Britain)*
Nastase I. *(Romania)*
Newcombe J.D. *(Australia)*
Okker T.S. *(Netherlands)*
Ramirez R. *(Mexico)*
Smith S.R. *(USA)*
Stockton R.L. *(USA)*

Holder: T Reid

For both the Boys' Singles *and* the Boys' Doubles Championships, the winners become the holders, for the year only, of a Cup presented by The All England Lawn Tennis and Croquet Club. The winners each receive a miniature Cup and the runners-up receive mementoes.

First Round	Second Round	Third Round	Quarter-Finals	Semi-Finals	Final
1. **Berdych, Tomas [1]** (CZE)	T.Berdych [1] ... 7/5 6/4	T.Berdych [1] ... 6/4 6/1	T.Berdych [1] ... 6/2 6/3	F.Mergea [6] ... 7/6(5) 7/6(5)	F.Mergea [6] 6/4 6/7(5) 6/4
2. Weber, Andreas (GER)					
3. Feeney, Adam (AUS)	A.Feeney ... 6/3 7/5				
4. Ouanna, Josselin (FRA)					
5. Cuellar, Jaime (ESA)	J.Goodall ... 7/6(5) 7/5	J.Goodall ... 6/1 7/6(5)			
6. Goodall, Joshua (GBR)					
(Q) 7. Kuznetsov, Alex (USA)	H-J.Suk [14] ... 6/7(5) 7/6(2) 6/4				
8. **Suk, Hyun-Joon [14]** (KOR)					
9. **Rosa, Bruno [11]** (BRA)	B.Rosa [11] ... 6/4 7/5	B.Rosa [11] ... 6/3 6/2	F.Mergea [6] ... 6/2 6/3		
10. Oudsema, Scott (USA)					
11. Muguruza, Jose Luis (ARU)	M.Kasiri ... 6/2 6/2				
(W) 12. Kasiri, Miles (GBR)					
13. Amado, Juan Pablo (ARG)	J.Amado ... 4/6 6/3 6/2	F.Mergea [6] ... 6/2 7/6(5)			
14. Tatuhey, Romano (NED)					
(Q) 15. Muller, Daniel (GER)	F.Mergea [6] ... 7/6(3) 6/1				
16. **Mergea, Florin [6]** (ROM)					
17. **Sela, Dudi [3]** (ISR)	D.Sela [3] ... 6/2 3/6 6/2	M.Zverev ... 6/4 6/4	L.Flores ... 7/6(8) 3/6 6/3	J-W.Tsonga [7] ... 6/2 6/4	
18. Rastogi, Karan (IND)					
19. Jarc, Rok (SLO)	M.Zverev ... 7/5 6/4				
20. Zverev, Mischa (GER)					
21. Chikhladze, Lado (GEO)	L.Flores ... 6/3 3/6 7/5	L.Flores ... 6/2 6/4			
22. Flores, Luis (MEX)					
(W) 23. Fass, Adam (USA)	D.Brewer [16] ... 6/2 6/2				
24. **Brewer, David [16]** (GBR)					
25. **Kwon, Chris [12]** (USA)	C.Kwon [12] ... 4/6 6/3 6/4	C.Kwon [12] ... 6/3 6/3	J-W.Tsonga [7] ... 6/1 7/6(5)		
26. Chirico, Jarrett (USA)					
(Q) 27. Kravchuk, Konstantin (RUS)	K.Kravchuk ... 7/6(1) 6/1				
28. Ungur, Adrian (ROM)					
(W) 29. Thomas, Guy (GBR)	H.Abid ... 6/3 7/6(4)	J-W.Tsonga [7] ... 6/2 6/4			
30. Abid, Haithem (TUN)					
(W) 31. Burn, Tom (GBR)	J-W.Tsonga [7] ... 7/6(5) 7/5				
32. **Tsonga, Jo-Wilfried [7]** (FRA)					
33. **Balazs, Gyorgy [5]** (HUN)	H.Tecau ... 6/4 6/2	H.Tecau ... 6/3 7/5	H.Tecau ... 6/4 6/4	H.Tecau ... 6/4 6/7(4) 6/1	C.Guccione [8] 6/3 6/4
34. Tecau, Horia (ROM)					
35. Mullings, Devin (BAH)	D.Mullings ... 7/6(3) 5/7 6/1				
36. Dev Varman, Somdev (IND)					
(Q) 37. Smeets, Robert (AUS)	R.Smeets ... 6-4, 6-3	R.Smeets ... 6/3 6/0			
38. Simmonds, Phillip (USA)					
(Q) 39. Steinberger, Peter (GER)	P.Steinberger ... 6/4 6/4				
40. **Murray, Andrew [10]** (GBR)					
41. **Gil, Frederico [15]** (POR)	F.Gil [15] ... 4/6 7/6(5) 6/4	F.Gil [15] ... 6/2 7/6(4)	B.Evans ... 6/1 6/2		
(Q) 42. Hutchins, Ross (GBR)					
(Q) 43. Lowe, Mat (GBR)	M.Lowe ... 6/4 6/7(2) 6/3				
44. Hadzic, Tomislav (CRO)					
45. Evans, Brendan (USA)	B.Evans ... 6/1 7/6(3)	B.Evans ... 7/6(7) 6/4			
(W) 46. Irwin, Richard (GBR)					
47. Kim, Sun-Yong Jr. (KOR)	M.Montcourt [4] ... 6/3 6/4				
48. **Montcourt, Mathieu [4]** (FRA)					
49. **Guccione, Chris [8]** (AUS)	C.Guccione [8] ... 6/3 6/4	C.Guccione [8] ... 6/3 6/2	C.Guccione [8] ... 6/3 6/4	C.Guccione [8] ... 7/6(3) 7/5	
50. Arevalo Gonzalez, Rafael (ESA)					
51. Figueroa, Pablo (SWE)	P.Figueroa ... 6/3 6/2				
(W) 52. Brown, Matthew (GBR)					
53. Cameron, Robert (USA)	S.Rieschick ... 6/1 6/0	S.Rieschick ... 7/5 3/6 10/8			
54. Rieschick, Sebastian (GER)					
55. Monfils, Gael (FRA)	G.Monfils ... 2/6 6/3 6/2				
56. Gimeno-Traver, Daniel [9] (ESP)					
57. **Kirche, Leonardo [13]** (BRA)	J.Baker ... 7/6(1) 6/3	J.Huta-Galung ... 6/3 6/2	B.Baker [2] ... 6/2 6/2		
58. Baker, Jamie (GBR)					
(Q) 59. Zivkovic, Denis (USA)	J.Huta-Galung ... 6/7(5) 6/4 7/5				
60. Huta-Galung, Jesse (NED)					
61. Fognini, Fabio (ITA)	F.Wolmarans ... 7/5 4/6 6/1	B.Baker [2] ... 7/5 4/6 6/3			
(W) 62. Wolmarans, Fritz (RSA)					
63. Stakhovsky, Sergiy (UKR)	B.Baker [2] ... 2/6 6/4 6/2				
64. **Baker, Brian [2]** (USA)					

Holders: F Mergea and H Tecau

First Round	Quarter-Finals	Semi-Finals	Final
1. **F.Mergea** (ROM) & **H.Tecau** (ROM) [1]	F.Mergea & H.Tecau [1] ... 7/6(5) 7/6(5)	F.Mergea & H.Tecau [1] ... 6/1 6/3	F.Mergea & H.Tecau [1] ... 6/3 7/5
2. H.Abid (TUN) & F.Wolmarans (RSA)			
3. A.Kuznetsov (USA) & M.Zverev (GER)	A.Kuznetsov & M.Zverev ... 6/3 6/4		
(W) 4. R.Hutchins (GBR) & G.Thomas (GBR)			
5. **G.Balazs** (HUN) & **D.Sela** (ISR) [4]	P.Figueroa & L.Flores ... 0/3 Ret'd.	A.Murray & T.Rushby ... 6/2 6/3	
6. P.Figueroa (SWE) & L.Flores (MEX)			
7. S.Dev Varman (IND) & K.Rastogi (IND)	A.Murray & T.Rushby ... 6/0 7/5		
8. A.Murray (GBR) & T.Rushby (GBR)			
9. A.Feeney (AUS) & C.Guccione (AUS)	A.Feeney & C.Guccione ... 7/5 3/6 11/9	A.Feeney & C.Guccione ... 6/3 7/6(1)	A.Feeney & C.Guccione ... 6/4 6/7 (3) 6/3
10. L.Chikhladze (GEO) & R.Jarc (SLO)			
11. C.Kwon (USA) & F.Gil (POR)	B.Evans & S.Oudsema [3] ... 5/7 7/6(6) 10/8		
12. **B.Evans** (USA) & **S.Oudsema** (USA) [3]			
13. T.Berdych (CZE) & S.Stakhovsky (UKR)	T.Berdych & S.Stakhovsky ... 6/3 6/4	B.Baker & P.Simmonds [2] ... 6/4 3/6 7/5	
14. J.Huta-Galung (NED) & R.Tatuhey (NED)			
15. D.Muller (GER) & S.Rieschick (GER)	B.Baker & P.Simmonds [2] ... 7/6(5) 6/2		
16. **B.Baker** (USA) & **P.Simmonds** (USA) [2]			

Winner: F.Mergea & H.Tecau [1] — 7/6(4) 7/5

Heavy type denotes seeded players. The figure in brackets against names denotes the order in which they have been seeded. (W) = Wild card. (Q) = Qualifier. (L) = Lucky loser.

The matches are the best of three sets

THE GIRLS' SINGLES CHAMPIONSHIP

Holder: Miss V Douchevina

First Round	Second Round	Third Round	Quarter-Finals	Semi-Finals	Final

1. **Rao, Sunitha [1]** ....(USA) — **Miss S.Rao [1]** 6/1 6/1
2. Szavay, Agnes ....(HUN)
(Q) 3. Andersson, Mari ....(SWE) — Miss T.Bacsinszky ....6/7(3) 6/1 6/3
4. Bacsinszky, Timea ....(SUI)

— **Miss S.Rao [1]** 6/3 6/0

5. Marama, Eden ....(NZL) — Miss E.Marama 6/2 6/4
6. Tangphong, Montinee.................(THA)
7. Tsutskova, Alyona ....(UKR) — **Miss S.Mirza [16]** 6/1 6/1
8. **Mirza, Sania [16]** ....(IND)

— Miss E.Marama 6/2 3/6 6/1

— **Miss S.Rao [1]** ....6/4 7/6(2)

9. **Hlavackova, Andrea [10]** ....(CZE) — **Miss A.Hlavackova [10]**...........6/1 6/1
(W) 10. Peterzan, Claire ....(GBR)
11. Moulton-Levy, Megan................(USA) — Miss A.Ivanovic 7/5 7/5
12. Ivanovic, Ana ....(YUG)

— Miss A.Ivanovic ....6/7(1) 6/3 8/6

(L) 13. Bunic, Tamara ....(CRO) — Miss K.Flipkens 6/3 6/2
14. Flipkens, Kirsten ....(BEL)
(Q) 15. Dubois, Stephanie ....(CAN) — **Miss A.Kleybanova [5]**....6/2 4/6 6/2
16. **Kleybanova, Alisa [5]** ....(RUS)

— Miss K.Flipkens ....6/3 6/7(4) 7/5

— Miss K.Flipkens 2/6 6/3 6/2

17. **Gajdosova, Jarmila [4]** ....(SVK) — **Miss J.Gajdosova [4]**.............6/2 6/1
(Q) 18. Gonzalez Penas, Adriana ....(ESP)
19. Rudman, Tarryn ....(RSA) — Miss K.Zoricic 6/0 6/0
20. Zoricic, Katarina ....(CAN)

— **Miss J.Gajdosova [4]**....6/2 6/1

21. Bondarenko, Katerina ....(UKR) — Miss K.Bondarenko 6/2 6/1
22. Marcio, Krysty ....(USA)
(Q) 23. Falcon, Megan ....(USA) — **Miss C.Dellacqua [14]**.........6/3 6/2
24. **Dellacqua, Casey [14]** ....(AUS)

— Miss K.Bondarenko 6/4 6/3

— **Miss J.Gajdosova [4]**...................6/1 6/4

(W) 25. **Golovin, Tatiana [12]** ....(FRA) — **Miss T.Golovin [12]**..............6/1 6/2
26. Cohen, Julia ....(USA)
(W) 27. Baker, Katharine ....(GBR) — Miss L.Giltinan 3/6 6/1
28. Giltinan, Lara ....(AUS)

— **Miss T.Golovin [12]**....6/0 6/2

29. Du, Rui ....(CHN) — Miss R.Du 6/3 6/4
30. Corovic, Vanja ....(YUG)
31. Vaidisova, Nicole ....(CZE) — Miss N.Vaidisova 5/7 6/4 6/3
32. **Fuda, Ryoko [8]** ....(JPN)

— Miss N.Vaidisova 6/1 6/0

— **Miss T.Golovin [12]**.....................6/3 6/4

33. **Baker, Ally [7]** ....(USA) — **Miss A.Baker [7]**..................7/5 6/3
(W) 34. Grady, Hannah ....(GBR)
35. Babos, Zsuzsanna ....(HUN) — Miss Z.Babos 6/3 6/3
36. Bhambri, Sanaa ....(IND)

— **Miss A.Baker [7]**........6/1 6/1

37. Peer, Shahar ....(ISR) — Miss S.Peer 4/6 6/4 6/1
38. Pavic, Nadja ....(CRO)
(Q) 39. Havartsova, Volha ....(BLR) — **Miss V.Lukic [9]**.................6/1 7/5
40. **Lukic, Vojislava [9]** ....(YUG)

— Miss S.Peer 5/7 6/1 6/3

— **Miss A.Baker [7]**..........................6/2 6/3

41. **Domachowska, Marta [15]** ......(POL) — Miss A.Tchakvetadze 3/6 6/2 6/3
(Q) 42. Tchakvetadze, Anna ....(RUS)
(W) 43. Bagshaw, Holly ....(GBR) — Miss B.Ko 6/4 3/6 6/2
44. Ko, Beier ....(CAN)

— Miss A.Tchakvetadze 6/4 6/2

45. Safarova, Lucie ....(CZE) — Miss L.Safarova ....7/6(5) 7/6(2)
46. Mitchell, Michelle ....(USA)
47. Czafikova, Kristina ....(SVK) — **Miss M.Krajicek [3]**.............6/4 3/6 6/1
48. **Krajicek, Michaela [3]** ....(NED)

— **Miss M.Krajicek [3]**....4/6 6/3 6/4

— Miss A.Tchakvetadze 1/6 6/4 8/6

49. **Bohmova, Katerina [6]** ....(CZE) — Miss K.O'Brien 2/6 6/0 7/5
(W) 50. O'Brien, Katie ....(GBR)
51. Gojnea, Madalina ....(ROM) — Miss M.Gojnea ....7/6(5) 1/6 6/0
52. Smolenakova, Linda ....(SVK)

— Miss K.O'Brien 6/4 6/2

53. Ichim, Iris ....(USA) — Miss I.Ichim 7/5 6/1
(W) 54. El Tabakh, Heidi ....(EGY)
(Q) 55. Ferguson, Sophie ....(AUS) — **Miss E.Laine [11]**...............6/1 6/4
56. **Laine, Emma [11]** ....(FIN)

— **Miss E.Laine [11]**.......6/1 6/3

— **Miss E.Laine [11]**........................6/1 7/5

57. **Kutuzova, Viktoria [13]** ....(UKR) — **Miss V.Kutuzova [13]**....7/5 6/7(6) 6/2
58. Kerber, Angelique ....(GER)
59. Kudryavtseva, Alla ....(RUS) — Miss A.Kudryavtseva ....7/6(6) 6/2
60. Sun, Sheng-Nan ....(CHN)

— Miss A.Kudryavtseva ....6/7(7) 7/6(5) 6/2

61. Vitayaviroj, Thassha ....(THA) — Miss M.Kawatoko 6/4 6/3
(Q) 62. Kawatoko, Moe ....(JPN)
(W) 63. Stoop, Georgie ....(GBR) — **Miss C.Gullickson [2]**..........6/2 6/3
64. **Gullickson, Carly [2]** ....(USA)

— **Miss C.Gullickson [2]**..6/1 6/2

— **Miss C.Gullickson [2]**..................2/6 6/3 6/4

— Miss S.Rao [1] .... Miss K.Flipkens 6/3 6/2

— Miss K.Flipkens 2/6 6/4 10/8

— **Miss J.Gajdosova [4]** 5/7 6/1 6/3

— Miss A.Tchakvetadze 1/6 7/5 6/3

— Miss E.Laine [11] 6/4 6/0

Miss K.Flipkens 2/6 6/4 10/8

Miss K.Flipkens 6/4 3/6 6/3

Miss A.Tchakvetadze 6/4 6/2

THE GIRLS' DOUBLES CHAMPIONSHIP

Holders: Miss E Clijsters and Miss B Strycova

First Round	Quarter-Finals	Semi-Finals	Final

1. **Miss J.Gajdosova (SVK) & Miss A.Hlavackova (CZE)** ...[1] — Miss A.Kleybanova & Miss S.Mirza
2. Miss A.Kleybanova (RUS) & Miss S.Mirza (IND) ....

— Miss A.Kleybanova & Miss S.Mirza ......7/6(7) 6/4

(W) 3. Miss K.O'Brien (GBR) & Miss G.Stoop (GBR) .... — Miss E.Laine & Miss N.Pavic
4. Miss E.Laine (FIN) & Miss N.Pavic (CRO) ....

— Miss E.Laine & Miss N.Pavic 6/1 6/2

— Miss A.Kleybanova & Miss S.Mirza 6/1 6/2

5. **Miss K.Bondarenko (UKR) & Miss A.Tsutskova (UKR)** ..[3] — **Miss K.Bondarenko & Miss A.Tsutskova [3]**
6. Miss M.Andersson (SWE) & Miss S.Ferguson (AUS) ....

— **Miss K.Bondarenko & Miss A.Tsutskova [3]** 6/0 6/4

7. Miss A.Baker (USA) & Miss I.Ichim (USA) .... — Miss A.Baker & Miss I.Ichim
8. Miss J.Cohen (USA) & Miss M.Mitchell (USA) ....

— Miss A.Baker & Miss I.Ichim 6/0 6/2

— Miss A.Baker & Miss I.Ichim ......6/3 7/6(1)

— Miss A.Kleybanova & Miss S.Mirza 6/3 5/7 6/4

9. Miss T.Bacsinszky (SUI) & Miss M.Gojnea (ROM) .... — Miss K.Bohmova & Miss M.Krajicek
10. Miss K.Bohmova (CZE) & Miss M.Krajicek (NED) ....

— Miss K.Bohmova & Miss M.Krajicek 7/5 6/3

11. Miss S.Bhambri (IND) & Miss L.Giltinan (AUS) .... — **Miss C.Dellacqua & Miss A.Szili [4]**
12. **Miss C.Dellacqua (AUS) & Miss A.Szili (AUS)** ...[4]

— **Miss C.Dellacqua & Miss A.Szili [4]** 6/1 6/4

— Miss K.Bohmova & Miss M.Krajicek ......6/3 7/6(3)

13. Miss M.Moulton-Levy (USA) & Miss K.Zoricic (CAN) .... — Miss M.Falcon & Miss A.Gonzalez Penas
14. Miss M.Falcon (USA) & Miss A.Gonzalez Penas (ESP) .....

— Miss M.Falcon & Miss A.Gonzalez Penas 6/2 6/2

15. Miss V.Havartsova (BLR) & Miss A.Kudryavtseva (RUS) ..... — Miss V.Havartsova & Miss A.Kudryavtseva
16. **Miss K.Czafikova (SVK) & Miss K.Flipkens (BEL)** ....[2]

— Miss V.Havartsova & Miss A.Kudryavtseva ......7/5 6/7(4) 11/9

— Miss M.Falcon & Miss A.Gonzalez Penas 7/5 6/3

— Miss K.Bohmova & Miss M.Krajicek 6/2 6/2

Miss A.Kleybanova & Miss S.Mirza 2/6 6/3 6/2

Champions and Runners-up

1877	S. W. Gore *W. C. Marshall*	1900	R. F. Doherty *S. H. Smith*	1927	H. Cochet *J. Borotra*	★ 1956	L. A. Hoad *K. R. Rosewall*	1979	B. Borg *R. Tanner*
1878	P. F. Hadow *S. W. Gore*	1901	A. W. Gore *R. F. Doherty*	1928	R. Lacoste *H. Cochet*	1957	L. A. Hoad *A. J. Cooper*	1980	B. Borg *J. P. McEnroe*
★ 1879	J. T. Hartley *V. St. L. Goold*	1902	H. L. Doherty *A. W. Gore*	★ 1929	H. Cochet *J. Borotra*	★ 1958	A. J. Cooper *N. A. Fraser*	1981	J. P. McEnroe *B. Borg*
1880	J. T. Hartley *H. F. Lawford*	1903	H. L. Doherty *F. L. Riseley*	1930	W. T. Tilden *W. Allison*	★ 1959	A. Olmedo *R. Laver*	1982	J. S. Connors *J. P. McEnroe*
1881	W. Renshaw *J. T. Hartley*	1904	H. L. Doherty *F. L. Riseley*	★ 1931	S. B. Wood *F. X. Shields*	★ 1960	N. A. Fraser *R. Laver*	1983	J. P. McEnroe *C. J. Lewis*
1882	W. Renshaw *E. Renshaw*	1905	H. L. Doherty *N. E. Brookes*	1932	H. E. Vines *H. W. Austin*	1961	R. Laver *C. R. McKinley*	1984	J. P. McEnroe *J. S. Connors*
1883	W. Renshaw *E. Renshaw*	1906	H. L. Doherty *F. L. Riseley*	1933	J. H. Crawford *H. E. Vines*	1962	R. Laver *M. F. Mulligan*	1985	B. Becker *K. Curren*
1884	W. Renshaw *H. F. Lawford*	★ 1907	N. E. Brookes *A. W. Gore*	1934	F. J. Perry *J. H. Crawford*	★ 1963	C. R. McKinley *F. S. Stolle*	1986	B. Becker *I. Lendl*
1885	W. Renshaw *H. F. Lawford*	★ 1908	A. W. Gore *H. Roper Barrett*	1935	F. J. Perry *G. von Cramm*	1964	R. Emerson *F. S. Stolle*	1987	P. Cash *I. Lendl*
1886	W. Renshaw *H. F. Lawford*	1909	A. W. Gore *M. J. G. Ritchie*	1936	F. J. Perry *G. von Cramm*	1965	R. Emerson *F. S. Stolle*	1988	S. Edberg *B. Becker*
★ 1887	H. F. Lawford *E. Renshaw*	1910	A. F. Wilding *A. W. Gore*	★ 1937	J. D. Budge *G. von Cramm*	1966	M. Santana *R. D. Ralston*	1989	B. Becker *S. Edberg*
1888	E. Renshaw *H. F. Lawford*	1911	A. F. Wilding *H. Roper Barrett*	1938	J. D. Budge *H. W. Austin*	1967	J. D. Newcombe *W. P. Bungert*	1990	S. Edberg *B. Becker*
1889	W. Renshaw *E. Renshaw*	1912	A. F. Wilding *A. W. Gore*	★ 1939	R. L. Riggs *E. T. Cooke*	1968	R. Laver *A. D. Roche*	1991	M. Stich *B. Becker*
1890	W. J. Hamilton *W. Renshaw*	1913	A. F. Wilding *M. E. McLoughlin*	★ 1946	Y. Petra *G. E. Brown*	1969	R. Laver *J. D. Newcombe*	1992	A. Agassi *G. Ivanisevic*
★ 1891	W. Baddeley *J. Pim*	1914	N. E. Brookes *A. F. Wilding*	1947	J. Kramer *T. Brown*	1970	J. D. Newcombe *K. R. Rosewall*	1993	P. Sampras *J. Courier*
1892	W. Baddeley *J. Pim*	1919	G. L. Patterson *N. E. Brookes*	★ 1948	R. Falkenburg *J. E. Bromwich*	1971	J. D. Newcombe *S. R. Smith*	1994	P. Sampras *G. Ivanisevic*
1893	J. Pim *W. Baddeley*	1920	W. T. Tilden *G. L. Patterson*	1949	F. R. Schroeder *J. Drobny*	★ 1972	S. R. Smith *I. Nastase*	1995	P. Sampras *B. Becker*
1894	J. Pim *W. Baddeley*	1921	W. T. Tilden *B. I. C. Norton*	★ 1950	B. Patty *F. A. Sedgman*	★ 1973	J. Kodes *A. Metreveli*	1996	R. Krajicek *M. Washington*
★ 1895	W. Baddeley *W. V. Eaves*	★† 1922	G. L. Patterson *R. Lycett*	1951	R. Savitt *K. McGregor*	1974	J. S. Connors *K. R. Rosewall*	1997	P. Sampras *C. Pioline*
1896	H. S. Mahony *W. Baddeley*	★ 1923	W. M. Johnston *F. T. Hunter*	1952	F. A. Sedgman *J. Drobny*	1975	A. R. Ashe *J. S. Connors*	1998	P. Sampras *G. Ivanisevic*
1897	R. F. Doherty *H. S. Mahony*	★ 1924	J. Borotra *R. Lacoste*	★ 1953	V. Seixas *K. Nielsen*	1976	B. Borg *I. Nastase*	1999	P. Sampras *A. Agassi*
1898	R. F. Doherty *H. L . Doherty*	1925	R. Lacoste *J. Borotra*	1954	J. Drobny *K. R. Rosewall*	1977	B. Borg *J. S. Connors*	2000	P. Sampras *P. Rafter*
1899	R. F. Doherty *A. W. Gore*	★ 1926	J. Borotra *H. Kinsey*	1955	T. Trabert *K. Nielsen*	1978	B. Borg *J. S.Connors*	2001	G. Ivanisevic *P. Rafter*
								2002	L. Hewitt *D. Nalbandian*

NOTE: For the years 1913, 1914 and 1919-23 inclusive the Championship Roll includes the 'World's Championship on Grass' granted to The Lawn Tennis Association by The International Lawn Tennis Federation. This title was then abolished and commencing in 1924 they became The Official Lawn Tennis Championships recognised by The International Lawn Tennis Federation.

Prior to 1922 the holders in the singles events and the gentlemen's doubles did not compete in The Championships but met the winners of these events in the Challenge Rounds.

† Challenge Round abolished; holders subsequently played through.   *The holder did not defend the title.

1884 Miss M. Watson *Miss L. Watson*	1906 Miss D. K. Douglass *Miss M. Sutton*	★1932 Mrs. F. S. Moody *Miss H. H. Jacobs*	★1959 Miss M. E. Bueno *Miss D. R. Hard*	1980 Mrs. R. Cawley *Mrs. J. M. Lloyd*
1885 Miss M. Watson *Miss B. Bingley*	1907 Miss M. Sutton *Mrs. Lambert Chambers*	1933 Mrs. F. S. Moody *Miss D. E. Round*	1960 Miss M. E. Bueno *Miss S. Reynolds*	★1981 Mrs. J. M. Lloyd *Miss H. Mandlikova*
1886 Miss B. Bingley *Miss M. Watson*	★1908 Mrs. A. Sterry *Miss A. M. Morton*	★1934 Miss D. E. Round *Miss H. H. Jacobs*	★1961 Miss A. Mortimer *Miss C. C. Truman*	1982 Miss M. Navratilova *Mrs. J. M. Lloyd*
1887 Miss L. Dod *Miss B. Bingley*	★1909 Miss D. P. Boothby *Miss A. M. Morton*	1935 Mrs. F. S. Moody *Miss H. H. Jacobs*	1962 Mrs. J. R. Susman *Mrs. V. Sukova*	1983 Miss M. Navratilova *Miss A. Jaeger*
1888 Miss L. Dod *Mrs. G. W. Hillyard*	1910 Mrs. Lambert Chambers *Miss D. P. Boothby*	★1936 Miss H. H. Jacobs *Frau. S. Sperling*	★1963 Miss M. Smith *Miss B. J. Moffitt*	1984 Miss M. Navratilova *Mrs. J. M. Lloyd*
★1889 Mrs. G. W. Hillyard *Miss L. Rice*	1911 Mrs. Lambert Chambers *Miss D. P. Boothby*	1937 Miss D. E. Round *Miss J. Jedrzejowska*	1964 Miss M. E. Bueno *Miss M. Smith*	1985 Miss M. Navratilova *Mrs. J. M. Lloyd*
★1890 Miss L. Rice *Miss M. Jacks*	★1912 Mrs. D. R. Larcombe *Mrs. A. Sterry*	★1938 Mrs. F. S. Moody *Miss H. H. Jacobs*	1965 Miss M. Smith *Miss M. E. Bueno*	1986 Miss M. Navratilova *Miss H. Mandlikova*
★1891 Miss L. Dod *Mrs. G. W. Hillyard*	★1913 Mrs. Lambert Chambers *Mrs. R. J. McNair*	★1939 Miss A. Marble *Miss K. E. Stammers*	1966 Mrs. L. W. King *Miss M. E. Bueno*	1987 Miss M. Navratilova *Miss S. Graf*
1892 Miss L. Dod *Mrs. G. W. Hillyard*	1914 Mrs. Lambert Chambers *Mrs. D. R. Larcombe*	★1946 Miss P. Betz *Miss L. Brough*	1967 Mrs. L. W. King *Mrs. P. F. Jones*	1988 Miss S. Graf *Miss M. Navratilova*
1893 Miss L. Dod *Mrs. G. W. Hillyard*	1919 Mlle. S. Lenglen *Mrs. Lambert Chambers*	★1947 Miss M. Osborne *Miss D. Hart*	1968 Mrs. L. W. King *Miss J. A. M. Tegart*	1989 Miss S. Graf *Miss M. Navratilova*
★1894 Mrs. G. W. Hillyard *Miss E. L. Austin*	1920 Mlle. S. Lenglen *Mrs. Lambert Chambers*	1948 Miss L. Brough *Miss D. Hart*	1969 Mrs. P. F. Jones *Mrs. L. W. King*	1990 Miss M. Navratilova *Miss Z. Garrison*
★1895 Miss C. Cooper *Miss H. Jackson*	1921 Mlle. S. Lenglen *Miss E. Ryan*	1949 Miss L. Brough *Mrs. W. du Pont*	★1970 Mrs. B. M. Court *Mrs. L. W. King*	1991 Miss S. Graf *Miss G. Sabatini*
1896 Miss C. Cooper *Mrs. W. H. Pickering*	†1922 Mlle. S. Lenglen *Mrs. F. Mallory*	1950 Miss L. Brough *Mrs. W. du Pont*	1971 Miss E. F. Goolagong *Mrs. B. M. Court*	1992 Miss S. Graf *Miss M. Seles*
1897 Mrs. G. W. Hillyard *Miss C. Cooper*	1923 Mlle. S. Lenglen *Miss K. McKane*	1951 Miss D. Hart *Miss S. Fry*	1972 Mrs. L. W. King *Miss E. F. Goolagong*	1993 Miss S. Graf *Miss J. Novotna*
★1898 Miss C. Cooper *Miss L. Martin*	1924 Miss K. McKane *Miss H. Wills*	1952 Miss M. Connolly *Miss L. Brough*	1973 Mrs. L. W. King *Miss C. M. Evert*	1994 Miss C. Martinez *Miss M. Navratilova*
1899 Mrs. G. W. Hillyard *Miss C. Cooper*	1925 Mlle. S. Lenglen *Miss J. Fry*	1953 Miss M. Connolly *Miss D. Hart*	1974 Miss C. M. Evert *Mrs. O. Morozova*	1995 Miss S. Graf *Miss A. Sanchez Vicario*
1900 Mrs. G. W. Hillyard *Miss C. Cooper*	1926 Mrs. L. A. Godfree *Sta. L. de Alvarez*	1954 Miss M. Connolly *Miss L. Brough*	1975 Mrs. L. W. King *Mrs. R. Cawley*	1996 Miss S. Graf *Miss A. Sanchez Vicario*
1901 Mrs. A. Sterry *Mrs. G. W. Hillyard*	1927 Miss H. Wills *Sta. L. de Alvarez*	★1955 Miss L. Brough *Mrs. J. G. Fleitz*	★1976 Miss C. M. Evert *Mrs. R. Cawley*	★1997 Miss M. Hingis *Miss J. Novotna*
1902 Miss M. E. Robb *Mrs. A. Sterry*	1928 Miss H. Wills *Sta. L. de Alvarez*	1956 Miss S. Fry *Miss A. Buxton*	1977 Miss S. V. Wade *Miss B. F. Stove*	1998 Miss J. Novotna *Miss N. Tauziat*
★1903 Miss D. K. Douglass *Miss E. W. Thomson*	1929 Miss H. Wills *Miss H. H. Jacobs*	★1957 Miss A. Gibson *Miss D. R. Hard*	1978 Miss M. Navratilova *Miss C. M. Evert*	1999 Miss L. A. Davenport *Miss S. Graf*
1904 Miss D. K. Douglass *Mrs. A. Sterry*	1930 Mrs. F. S. Moody *Miss E. Ryan*	1958 Miss A. Gibson *Miss A. Mortimer*	1979 Miss M. Navratilova *Mrs. J. M. Lloyd*	2000 Miss V. Williams *Miss L. A. Davenport*
1905 Miss M. Sutton *Miss D. K. Douglass*	★1931 Fraulein C. Aussem *Fraulein H. Krahwinkel*			2001 Miss V. Williams *Miss J. Henin*
				2002 Miss S. Williams *Miss V. Williams*

MAIDEN NAMES OF LADY CHAMPIONS *(In the tables the following have been recorded in both married and single identities)*

Mrs. R. Cawley...........Miss E. F. Goolagong	Mrs. G. W. Hillyard...........Miss B. Bingley	Mrs. L. E. G. Price...........Miss S. Reynolds	
Mrs. Lambert Chambers...........Miss D. K. Douglass	Mrs. P. F. Jones...........Miss A. S. Haydon	Mrs. G. E. Reid...........Miss K. Melville	
Mrs. B. M. Court...........Miss M. Smith	Mrs. L. W. King...........Miss B. J. Moffitt	Mrs. P. D. Smylie...........Miss E. M. Sayers	
Mrs. B. C. Covell...........Miss P. L. Howkins	Mrs. M. R. King...........Miss P. E. Mudford	Frau. S. Sperling...........Fraulein H. Krahwinkel	
Mrs. D. E. Dalton...........Miss J. A. M. Tegart	Mrs. D. R. Larcombe...........Miss E. W. Thomson	Mrs. A. Sterry...........Miss C. Cooper	
Mrs. W. du Pont...........Miss M. Osborne	Mrs. J. M. Lloyd...........Miss C. M. Evert	Mrs. J. R. Susman...........Miss K. Hantze	
Mrs. L. A. Godfree...........Miss K. McKane	Mrs. F. S. Moody...........Miss H. Wills		
Mrs. H. F. Gourlay Cawley...........Miss H. F. Gourlay	Mrs. O. Morozova...........Miss O. Morozova		

GENTLEMEN'S DOUBLES

1879 L. R. Erskine and H. F. Lawford
F. Durant and G. E. Tabor
1880 W. Renshaw and E. Renshaw
O. E. Woodhouse and C. J. Cole
1881 W. Renshaw and E. Renshaw
W. J. Down and H. Vaughan
1882 J. T. Hartley and R. T. Richardson
J. G. Horn and C. B. Russell
1883 C. W. Grinstead and C. E. Welldon
C. B. Russell and R. T. Milford
1884 W. Renshaw and E. Renshaw
E. W. Lewis and E. L Williams
1885 W. Renshaw and E. Renshaw
C. E. Farrer and A. J. Stanley
1886 W. Renshaw and E. Renshaw
C. E. Farrer and A. J. Stanley
1887 P. Bowes-Lyon and H. W. W. Wilberforce
J. H. Crispe and E. Barratt Smith
1888 W. Renshaw and E. Renshaw
P. Bowes-Lyon and H. W. W. Wilberforce
1889 W. Renshaw and E. Renshaw
E. W. Lewis and G. W. Hillyard
1890 J. Pim and F. O. Stoker
E. W. Lewis and G. W. Hillyard
1891 W. Baddeley and H. Baddeley
J. Pim and F. O. Stoker
1892 H. S. Barlow and E. W. Lewis
W. Baddeley and H. Baddeley
1893 J. Pim and F. O. Stoker
E. W. Lewis and H. S. Barlow
1894 W. Baddeley and H. Baddeley
H. S. Barlow and C. H. Martin
1895 W. Baddeley and H. Baddeley
E. W. Lewis and W. V. Eaves
1896 W. Baddeley and H. Baddeley
R. F. Doherty and H. A. Nisbet
1897 R. F. Doherty and H. L. Doherty
W. Baddeley and H. Baddeley
1898 R. F. Doherty and H. L . Doherty
H. A. Nisbet and C. Hobart
1899 R. F. Doherty and H. L. Doherty
H. A. Nisbet and C. Hobart
1900 R. F. Doherty and H. L. Doherty
H. Roper Barrett and H. A. Nisbet
1901 R. F. Doherty and H. L. Doherty
Dwight Davis and Holcombe Ward
1902 S. H. Smith and F. L. Riseley
R. F. Doherty and H. L. Doherty
1903 R. F. Doherty and H. L. Doherty
S. H. Smith and F. L. Riseley
1904 R. F. Doherty and H. L. Doherty
S. H. Smith and F. L. Riseley
1905 R. F. Doherty and H. L. Doherty
S. H. Smith and F. L. Riseley
1906 S. H. Smith and F. L. Riseley
R. F. Doherty and H. L. Doherty
1907 N. E. Brookes and A. F. Wilding
B. C. Wright and K. H. Behr
1908 A. F. Wilding and M. J. G. Ritchie
A. W. Gore and H. Roper Barrett
1909 A. W. Gore and H. Roper Barrett
S. N. Doust and H. A. Parker
1910 A. F. Wilding and M. J. G. Ritchie
A. W. Gore and H. Roper Barrett
1911 M. Decugis and A. H. Gobert
M. J. G. Ritchie and A. F. Wilding
1912 H. Roper Barrett and C. P. Dixon
M. Decugis and A. H. Gobert
1913 H. Roper Barrett and C. P. Dixon
F. W. Rahe and H. Kleinschroth
1914 N. E. Brookes and A. F. Wilding
H. Roper Barrett and C. P. Dixon
1919 R. V. Thomas and P. O'Hara-Wood
R. Lycett and R. W. Heath
1920 R. N. Williams and C. S. Garland
A. R. F. Kingscote and J. C. Parke
1921 R. Lycett and M. Woosnam
F. G. Lowe and A. H. Lowe
1922 R. Lycett and J. O. Anderson
G. L. Patterson and P. O'Hara-Wood
1923 R. Lycett and L. A. Godfree
Count de Gomar and E. Flaquer
1924 F. T. Hunter and V. Richards
R. N. Williams and W. M. Washburn
1925 J. Borotra and R. Lacoste
J. Hennessey and R. Casey
1926 H. Cochet and J. Brugnon
V. Richards and H. Kinsey
1927 F. T. Hunter and W. T. Tilden
J. Brugnon and H. Cochet
1928 H. Cochet and J. Brugnon
G. L. Patterson and J. B. Hawkes
1929 W. Allison and J. Van Ryn
J. C. Gregory and I. G. Collins
1930 W. Allison and J. Van Ryn
J. H. Doeg and G. M. Lott
1931 G. M Lott and J. Van Ryn
H. Cochet and J. Brugnon
1932 J. Borotra and J. Brugnon
G. P. Hughes and F. J. Perry
1933 J. Borotra and J. Brugnon
R. Nunoi and J. Satoh
1934 G. M. Lott and L. R. Stoefen
J. Borotra and J. Brugnon
1935 J. H. Crawford and A. K. Quist
W. Allison and J. Van Ryn
1936 G. P. Hughes and C. R. D. Tuckey
C. E. Hare and F. H. D. Wilde
1937 J. D. Budge and G. Mako
G. P. Hughes and C. R. D. Tuckey
1938 J. D. Budge and G. Mako
H. Henkel and G. von Metaxa
1939 R. L. Riggs and E. T. Cooke
C. E. Hare and F. H. D. Wilde
1946 T. Brown and J. Kramer
G. E. Brown and D. Pails
1947 R. Falkenburg and J. Kramer
A. J. Mottram and O. W. Sidwell
1948 J. E. Bromwich and F. A. Sedgman
T. Brown and G. Mulloy
1949 R. Gonzales and F. Parker
G. Mulloy and F. R. Schroeder
1950 J. E. Bromwich and A. K. Quist
G. E. Brown and O. W. Sidwell
1951 K. McGregor and F. A. Sedgman
J. Drobny and E. W. Sturgess
1952 K. McGregor and F. A. Sedgman
V. Seixas and E. W. Sturgess
1953 L. A. Hoad and K. R. Rosewall
R. N. Hartwig and M. G. Rose
1954 R. N. Hartwig and M. G. Rose
V. Seixas and T. Trabert
1955 R. N. Hartwig and L. A. Hoad
N. A. Fraser and K. R. Rosewall
1956 L. A. Hoad and K. R. Rosewall
N. Pietrangeli and O. Sirola
1957 G. Mulloy and B. Patty
N. A. Fraser and L. A. Hoad
1958 S. Davidson and U. Schmidt
A. J. Cooper and N. A. Fraser
1959 R. Emerson and N. A. Fraser
R. Laver and R. Mark
1960 R. H. Osuna and R. D. Ralston
M. G. Davies and R. K. Wilson
1961 R. Emerson and N. A. Fraser
R. A. J. Hewitt and F. S. Stolle
1962 R. A. J. Hewitt and F. S. Stolle
B. Jovanovic and N. Pilic
1963 R. H. Osuna and A. Palafox
J. C. Barclay and P. Darmon
1964 R. A. J. Hewitt and F. S. Stolle
R. Emerson and K. N. Fletcher
1965 J. D. Newcombe and A. D. Roche
K. N. Fletcher and R. A. J. Hewitt
1966 K. N. Fletcher and J. D. Newcombe
W. W. Bowrey and O. K. Davidson
1967 R. A. J. Hewitt and F. D. McMillan
R. Emerson and K. N. Fletcher
1968 J. D. Newcombe and A. D. Roche
K. R. Rosewall and F. S. Stolle
1969 J. D. Newcombe and A. D. Roche
T. S. Okker and M. C. Reissen
1970 J. D. Newcombe and A. D. Roche
K. R. Rosewall and F. S. Stolle
1971 R. S. Emerson and R. G. Laver
A. R. Ashe and R. D. Ralston
1972 R. A. J. Hewitt and F. D. McMillan
S. R. Smith and E. J. van Dillen
1973 J. S. Connors and I. Nastase
J. R. Cooper and N. A. Fraser
1974 J. D. Newcombe and A. D. Roche
R. C. Lutz and S. R. Smith
1975 V. Gerulaitis and A. Mayer
C. Dowdeswell and A. J. Stone
1976 B. E. Gottfried and R. Ramirez
R. L. Case and G. Masters
1977 R. L. Case and G. Masters
J. G. Alexander and P. C. Dent
1978 R. A. J. Hewitt and F. D. McMillan
P. Fleming and J. P. McEnroe
1979 P. Fleming and J. P . McEnroe
B. E. Gottfried and R. Ramirez
1980 P. McNamara and P. McNamee
R. C. Lutz and S. R. Smith
1981 P. Fleming and J. P. McEnroe
R. C. Lutz and S. R. Smith
1982 P. McNamara and P. McNamee
P. Fleming and J. P. McEnroe
1983 P. Fleming and J. P McEnroe
T. E. Gullikson and T. R. Gullikson
1984 P. Fleming and J. P. McEnroe
P. Cash and P. McNamee
1985 H. P. Guenthardt and B. Taroczy
P. Cash and J. B. Fitzgerald
1986 J. Nystrom and M. Wilander
G. Donnelly and P. Fleming
1987 K. Flach and R. Seguso
S. Casal and E. Sanchez
1988 K. Flach and R. Seguso
J. B. Fitzgerald and A. Jarryd
1989 J. B. Fitzgerald and A. Jarryd
R. Leach and J. Pugh
1990 R. Leach and J. Pugh
P. Aldrich and D. T. Visser
1991 J. B. Fitzgerald and A. Jarryd
J. Frana and L. Lavalle
1992 J. P. McEnroe and M. Stich
J. Grabb and R. A. Reneberg
1993 T. A. Woodbridge and M. Woodforde
G. Connell and P. Galbraith
1994 T. A. Woodbridge and M. Woodforde
G. Connell and P. Galbraith
1995 T. A. Woodbridge and M. Woodforde
R. Leach and S. Melville
1996 T. A. Woodbridge and M. Woodforde
B. Black and G. Connell
1997 T. A. Woodbridge and M. Woodforde
J. Eltingh and P. Haarhuis
1998 J. Eltingh and P. Haarhuis
T. A. Woodbridge and M. Woodforde
1999 M. Bhupathi and L. Paes
P. Haarhuis and J. Palmer
2000 T. A. Woodbridge and M. Woodforde
P. Haarhuis and S. Stolle
2001 D. Johnson and J. Palmer
J. Novak and D. Rikl
2002 J. Bjorkman and T. A Woodbridge
M. Knowles and D. Nestor

LADIES' DOUBLES

1913 Mrs. R. J. McNair and Miss D. P. Boothby
Mrs. A. Sterry and Mrs. Lambert Chambers
1914 Miss E. Ryan and Miss A. M. Morton
Mrs. D. R. Larcombe and Mrs. F. J. Hannam
1919 Mlle. S. Lenglen and Miss E. Ryan
Mrs. Lambert Chambers and Mrs. D. R. Larcombe
1920 Mlle. S. Lenglen and Miss E. Ryan
Mrs. Lambert Chambers and Mrs. D. R. Larcombe
1921 Mlle. S. Lenglen and Miss E. Ryan
Mrs. A. E. Beamish and Mrs. G. E. Peacock
1922 Mlle. S. Lenglen and Miss E. Ryan
Mrs. A. D. Stocks and Miss K. McKane
1923 Mlle. S. Lenglen and Miss E. Ryan
Miss J. Austin and Miss E. L. Colyer
1924 Mrs. H. Wightman and Miss H. Wills
Mrs. B. C. Covell and Miss K. McKane
1925 Mlle. S. Lenglen and Miss E. Ryan
Mrs. A. V. Bridge and Mrs. C. G. McIlquham
1926 Miss E. Ryan and Miss M. K. Browne
Mrs. L. A. Godfree and Miss E. L. Colyer
1927 Miss H. Wills and Miss E. Ryan
Miss E. L. Heine and Mrs. G. E. Peacock
1928 Mrs. Holcroft-Watson and Miss P. Saunders
Miss E. H. Harvey and Miss E. Bennett
1929 Mrs. Holcroft-Watson and Mrs. L.R.C. Michell
Mrs. B. C. Covell and Mrs. D. C. Shepherd-Barron
1930 Mrs. F. S. Moody and Miss E. Ryan
Miss E. Cross and Miss S. Palfrey
1931 Mrs.D.C. Shepherd-Barron and Miss P.E. Mudford
Mlle. D. Metaxa and Mlle. J. Sigart
1932 Mlle. D. Metaxa and Mlle. J. Sigart
Miss E. Ryan and Miss H. H. Jacobs
1933 Mme. R. Mathieu and Miss E. Ryan
Miss F. James and Miss A. M. Yorke
1934 Mme. R. Mathieu and Miss E. Ryan
Mrs. D. Andrus and Mme. S. Henrotin
1935 Miss F. James and Miss K. E. Stammers
Mme. R. Mathieu and Frau. S. Sperling
1936 Miss F. James and Miss K. E. Stammers
Mrs. S. P. Fabyan and Miss H. H. Jacobs
1937 Mme. R. Mathieu and Miss A. M. Yorke
Mrs. M. R. King and Mrs. J. B. Pittman
1938 Mrs. S. P. Fabyan and Miss A. Marble
Mme. R. Mathieu and Miss A. M. Yorke
1939 Mrs S. P. Fabyan and Miss A. Marble
Miss H. H. Jacobs and Miss A. M. Yorke
1946 Miss L. Brough and Miss M. Osborne
Miss P. Betz and Miss D. Hart
1947 Miss D. Hart and Mrs. P. C. Todd
Miss L. Brough and Miss M. Osborne
1948 Miss L. Brough and Mrs. W. du Pont
Miss D. Hart and Mrs. P. C. Todd
1949 Miss L. Brough and Mrs. W. du Pont
Miss G. Moran and Mrs. P. C. Todd
1950 Miss L. Brough and Mrs. W. du Pont
Miss S. Fry and Miss D. Hart
1951 Miss S. Fry and Miss D. Hart
Miss L. Brough and Mrs. W. du Pont
1952 Miss S. Fry and Miss D. Hart
Miss L. Brough and Miss M. Connolly
1953 Miss S. Fry and Miss D. Hart
Miss M. Connolly and Miss J. Sampson
1954 Miss L. Brough and Mrs. W. du Pont
Miss S. Fry and Miss D. Hart
1955 Miss A. Mortimer and Miss J. A. Shilcock
Miss S. J. Bloomer and Miss P. E. Ward
1956 Miss A. Buxton and Miss A. Gibson
Miss F. Muller and Miss D. G. Seeney
1957 Miss A. Gibson and Miss D. R. Hard
Mrs. K. Hawton and Mrs. T. D. Long
1958 Miss M. E. Bueno and Miss A. Gibson
Mrs. W. du Pont and Miss M. Varner
1959 Miss J. Arth and Miss D. R. Hard
Mrs. J. G. Fleitz and Miss C. C. Truman
1960 Miss M. E. Bueno and Miss D. R. Hard
Miss S. Reynolds and Miss R. Schuurman
1961 Miss K. Hantze and Miss B. J. Moffitt
Miss J. Lehane and Miss M. Smith
1962 Miss B. J. Moffitt and Mrs. J. R. Susman
Mrs. L. E. G. Price and Miss R. Schuurman
1963 Miss M. E. Bueno and Miss D. R. Hard
Miss R. A. Ebbern and Miss M. Smith
1964 Miss M. Smith and Miss L. R. Turner
Miss B. J. Moffitt and Mrs. J. R. Susman
1965 Miss M. E. Bueno and Miss B. J. Moffitt
Miss F. Durr and Miss J. Lieffrig
1966 Miss M. E. Bueno and Miss N. Richey
Miss M. Smith and Miss J. A. M. Tegart
1967 Miss R. Casals and Mrs. L. W. King
Miss M. E. Bueno and Miss N. Richey
1968 Miss R. Casals and Mrs. L. W. King
Miss F. Durr and Mrs. P. F. Jones
1969 Mrs. B. M. Court and Miss J. A. M. Tegart
Miss P. S. A. Hogan and Miss M. Michel
1970 Miss R. Casals and Mrs. L. W. King
Miss F. Durr and Miss S. V. Wade
1971 Miss R. Casals and Mrs. L. W. King
Mrs. B. M. Court and Miss E. F. Goolagong
1972 Mrs. L. W. King and Miss B. F. Stove
Mrs. D. E. Dalton and Miss F. Durr
1973 Miss R. Casals and Mrs. L. W. King
Miss F. Durr and Miss B. F. Stove
1974 Miss E. F. Goolagong and Miss M. Michel
Miss H. F. Gourlay and Miss K. M. Krantzcke
1975 Miss A. Kiyomura and Miss K. Sawamatsu
Miss F. Durr and Miss B. F. Stove
1976 Miss C. M. Evert and Miss M. Navratilova
Mrs. L. W. King and Miss B. F. Stove
1977 Mrs. H. F. Gourlay Cawley and Miss J. C. Russell
Miss M. Navratilova and Miss B. F . Stove
1978 Mrs. G. E. Reid and Miss. W. M. Turnbull
Miss M. Jausovec and Miss V. Ruzici
1979 Mrs. L. W. King and Miss M. Navratilova
Miss B. F. Stove and Miss W. M. Turnbull
1980 Miss K. Jordan and Miss A. E. Smith
Miss R. Casals and Miss W. M. Turnbull
1981 Miss M. Navratilova and Miss P. H. Shriver
Miss K. Jordan and Miss A. E. Smith
1982 Miss M. Navratilova and Miss P. H. Shriver
Miss K. Jordan and Miss A. E. Smith
1983 Miss M. Navratilova and Miss P. H. Shriver
Miss R. Casals and Miss W. M. Turnbull
1984 Miss M. Navratilova and Miss P. H. Shriver
Miss K. Jordan and Miss A. E. Smith
1985 Miss K. Jordan and Mrs. P. D. Smylie
Miss M. Navratilova and Miss P. H. Shriver
1986 Miss M. Navratilova and Miss P. H. Shriver
Miss H. Mandlikova and Miss W. M. Turnbull
1987 Miss C. Kohde-Kilsch and Miss H. Sukova
Miss B. Nagelsen and Mrs. P. D. Smylie
1988 Miss S. Graf and Miss G. Sabatini
Miss L. Savchenko and Miss N. Zvereva
1989 Miss J. Novotna and Miss H. Sukova
Miss L. Savchenko and Miss N. Zvereva
1990 Miss J. Novotna and Miss H. Sukova
Miss K. Jordan and Mrs. P. D. Smylie
1991 Miss L. Savchenko and Miss N. Zvereva
Miss G. Fernandez and Miss J. Novotna
1992 Miss G. Fernandez and Miss N. Zvereva
Miss J. Novotna and Mrs. L. Savchenko-Neiland
1993 Miss G. Fernandez and Miss N. Zvereva
Mrs. L. Neiland and Miss J. Novotna
1994 Miss G. Fernandez and Miss N. Zvereva
Miss J. Novotna and Miss A. Sanchez Vicario
1995 Miss J. Novotna and Miss A. Sanchez Vicario
Miss G. Fernandez and Miss N. Zvereva
1996 Miss M. Hingis and Miss H. Sukova
Miss M. J. McGrath and Mrs. L. Neiland
1997 Miss G. Fernandez and Miss N. Zvereva
Miss N. J. Arendt and Miss M. M. Bollegraf
1998 Miss M. Hingis and Miss J. Novotna
Miss L. A. Davenport and Miss N. Zvereva
1999 Miss L. A. Davenport and Miss C. Morariu
Miss M. de Swardt and Miss E. Tatarkova
2000 Miss S. Williams and Miss V. Williams
Mrs J. Halard–Decugis and Miss A. Sugiyama
2001 Miss L. M. Raymond and Miss R. P. Stubbs
Miss K. Clijsters and Miss A. Sugiyama
2002 Miss S. Williams and Miss V. Williams
Miss V. Ruano Pascual and Miss P. Suarez

MIXED DOUBLES

1913 H. Crisp and Mrs. C. O. Tuckey
J. C. Parke and Mrs. D. R. Larcombe
1914 J. C. Parke and Mrs. D.R. Larcombe
A. F. Wilding and Mlle. M. Broquedis
1919 R. Lycett and Miss E. Ryan
A. D. Prebble and Mrs. Lambert Chambers
1920 G. L. Patterson and Mlle. S. Lenglen
R. Lycett and Miss E. Ryan
1921 R. Lycett and Miss E. Ryan
M. Woosnam and Miss P. L. Howkins
1922 P. O'Hara-Wood and Mlle. S. Lenglen
R. Lycett and Miss E. Ryan
1923 R. Lycett and Miss E. Ryan
L. S. Deane and Mrs. D. C. Shepherd-Barron
1924 J. B. Gilbert and Miss K. McKane
L. A. Godfree and Mrs. D. C. Shepherd-Barron
1925 J. Borotra and Mlle. S. Lenglen
H. L. de Morpurgo and Miss E. Ryan
1926 L. A. Godfree and Mrs. L. A. Godfree
H. Kinsey and Miss M. K. Browne
1927 F.T. Hunter and Miss E. Ryan
L. A. Godfree and Mrs. L. A. Godfree
1928 P. D. B. Spence and Miss E. Ryan
J. Crawford and Miss D. Akhurst
1929 F. T. Hunter and Miss H. Wills
I. G. Collins and Miss J. Fry
1930 J. H. Crawford and Miss E. Ryan
D. Prenn and Fraulein H. Krahwinkel
1931 G. M. Lott and Mrs. L. A. Harper
I. G. Collins and Miss J. C. Ridley
1932 E. Maier and Miss E. Ryan
H. C. Hopman and Mlle. J. Sigart
1933 G. von Cramm and Fraulein H. Krahwinkel
N. G. Farquharson and Miss M. Heeley
1934 R. Miki and Miss D. E. Round
H. W. Austin and Mrs D. C. Shepherd-Barron
1935 F. J. Perry and Miss D. E. Round
H. C. Hopman and Mrs. H. C. Hopman
1936 F. J. Perry and Miss D. E. Round
J. D. Budge and Mrs. S. P. Fabyan

1937 J. D. Budge and Miss A. Marble
Y. Petra and Mme. R. Mathieu
1938 J. D. Budge and Miss A. Marble
H. Henkel and Mrs. S. P. Fabyan
1939 R. L. Riggs and Miss A. Marble
F. H. D. Wilde and Miss N. B. Brown
1946 T. Brown and Miss L. Brough
G. E. Brown and Miss D. Bundy
1947 J. E. Bromwich and Miss L. Brough
C. F. Long and Mrs. N. M. Bolton
1948 J. E. Bromwich and Miss L. Brough
F. A. Sedgman and Miss D. Hart
1949 E. W. Sturgess and Mrs. S. P. Summers
J. E. Bromwich and Miss L. Brough
1950 E. W. Sturgess and Miss L. Brough
G. E. Brown and Mrs. P. C. Todd
1951 F. A. Sedgman and Miss D. Hart
M. G. Rose and Mrs. N. M. Bolton
1952 F. A. Sedgman and Miss D. Hart
E. Morea and Miss D. Fry
1953 V. Seixas and Miss D. Hart
E. Morea and Miss S. Fry
1954 V. Seixas and Miss D. Hart
K. R. Rosewall and Mrs. W. du Pont
1955 V. Seixas and Miss D. Hart
E. Morea and Miss L. Brough
1956 V. Seixas and Miss S. Fry
G. Mulloy and Miss A. Gibson
1957 M. G. Rose and Miss D. R. Hard
N. A. Fraser and Miss A. Gibson
1958 R. N. Howe and Miss L. Coghlan
K. Nielsen and Miss A. Gibson
1959 R. Laver and Miss D. R. Hard
N. A. Fraser and Miss M. E. Bueno
1960 R. Laver and Miss D. R. Hard
R. N. Howe and Miss M. E. Bueno
1961 F. S. Stolle and Miss L. R. Turner
R. N. Howe and Miss E. Buding
1962 N. A. Fraser and Mrs. W. du Pont
R. D. Ralston and Miss A. S. Haydon

1963 K. N. Fletcher and Miss M. Smith
R. A. J. Hewitt and Miss D. R. Hard
1964 F. S. Stolle and Miss L. R. Turner
K. N. Fletcher and Miss M. Smith
1965 K. N. Fletcher and Miss M. Smith
A. D. Roche and Miss J. A. M. Tegart
1966 K. N. Fletcher and Miss M. Smith
R. D. Ralston and Mrs. L. W. King
1967 O. K. Davidson and Mrs. L. W. King
K. N. Fletcher and Miss M. E. Bueno
1968 K. N. Fletcher and Mrs. B. M. Court
A. Metreveli and Miss O. Morozova
1969 F. S. Stolle and Mrs. P. F. Jones
A. D. Roche and Miss J. A. M. Tegart
1970 I. Nastase and Miss R. Casals
A. Metreveli and Miss O. Morozova
1971 O. K. Davidson and Mrs. L. W. King
M. C. Riessen and Mrs. B. M. Court
1972 I. Nastase and Miss R. Casals
K. G. Warwick and Miss E. F. Goolagong
1973 O. K. Davidson and Mrs. L. W. King
R. Ramirez and Miss J. S. Newberry
1974 O. K. Davidson and Mrs. L. W. King
M. J. Farrell and Miss L. J. Charles
1975 M. C. Riessen and Mrs. B. M. Court
A. J. Stone and Miss B. F. Stove
1976 A. D. Roche and Miss F. Durr
R. L. Stockton and Miss R. Casals
1977 R. A. J. Hewitt and Miss G. R. Stevens
F. D. McMillan and Miss B. F. Stove
1978 F. D. McMillan and Miss B. F. Stove
R. O. Ruffels and Mrs. L. W. King
1979 R. A. J. Hewitt and Miss G. R. Stevens
F. D. McMillan and Miss B. F. Stove
1980 J. R. Austin and Miss T. Austin
M. R. Edmondson and Miss D. L. Fromholtz
1981 F. D. McMillan and Miss B. F. Stove
J. R. Austin and Miss T. Austin
1982 K. Curren and Miss A. E. Smith
J. M. Lloyd and Miss W. M. Turnbull

1983 J. M. Lloyd and Miss W. M. Turnbull
S. Denton and Mrs. L. W. King
1984 J. M. Lloyd and Miss W. M. Turnbull
S. Denton and Miss K. Jordan
1985 P. McNamee and Miss M. Navratilova
J. B. Fitzgerald and Mrs. P. D. Smylie
1986 K. Flach and Miss K. Jordan
H. P. Guenthardt and Miss M. Navratilova
1987 M. J. Bates and Miss J. M. Durie
D. Cahill and Miss N. Provis
1988 S. E. Stewart and Miss Z. L. Garrison
K. Jones and Mrs. S. W. Magers
1989 J. Pugh and Miss J. Novotna
M. Kratzmann and Miss J. M. Byrne
1990 R. Leach and Miss Z. L. Garrison
J. B. Fitzgerald and Mrs P. D. Smylie
1991 J. B. Fitzgerald and Mrs. P. D. Smylie
J. Pugh and Miss N. Zvereva
1992 C. Suk and Mrs L. Savchenko-Neiland
J. Eltingh and Miss M. Oremans
1993 M. Woodforde and Miss M. Navratilova
T. Nijssen and Miss M. M. Bollegraf
1994 T. A. Woodbridge and Miss H. Sukova
T. J. Middleton and Miss L. M. McNeil
1995 J. Stark and Miss M. Navratilova
C. Suk and Miss G. Fernandez
1996 C. Suk and Miss H. Sukova
M. Woodforde and Mrs. L. Neiland
1997 C. Suk and Miss H. Sukova
A. Olhovskiy and Mrs L. Neiland
1998 M. Mirnyi and Miss S. Williams
M. Bhupathi and Miss M. Lucic
1999 L. Paes and Miss L.M. Raymond
J. Bjorkman and Miss A. Kournikova
2000 D. Johnson and Miss K. Po
L. Hewitt and Miss K. Clijsters
2001 L. Friedl and Miss D. Hantuchova
M. Bryan and Mrs L. Huber
2002 M. Bhupathi and Miss E. Likhovtseva
K. Ullyett and Miss D. Hantuchova

THE JUNIOR CHAMPIONSHIP ROLL

BOYS' SINGLES

1947 K. Nielsen (Denmark)
1948 S. Stockenberg (Sweden)
1949 S. Stockenberg (Sweden)
1950 J.A.T. Horn (G.B.)
1951 J. Kupferburger (S.A.)
1952 R. K. Wilson (G.B.)
1953 W. A. Knight (G.B.)
1954 R. Krishnan (India)
1955 M. P. Hann (G.B.)
1956 R. Holmberg (U.S.A.)
1957 J. I. Tattersall (G.B.)
1958 E. Buchholz (U.S.A.)
1959 T. Lejus (U.S.S.R.)
1960 A. R. Mandelstam (S.A.)

1961 C. E. Graebner (U.S.A.)
1962 S. Matthews (G.B.)
1963 N. Kalogeropoulos (Greece)
1964 I. El Shafei (U.A.R.)
1965 V. Korotkov (U.S.S.R.)
1966 V. Korotkov (U.S.S.R.)
1967 M. Orantes (Spain)
1968 J. G. Alexander (Australia)
1969 B. Bertram (S.A.)
1970 B. Bertram (S.A.)
1971 R. Kreiss (U.S.A.)
1972 B. Borg (Sweden)
1973 W. Martin (U.S.A.)
1974 W. Martin (U.S.A.)

1975 C. J. Lewis (N.Z.)
1976 H. Guenthardt (Switzerland)
1977 V. A. Winitsky (U.S.A.)
1978 I. Lendl (Czechoslovakia)
1979 R. Krishnan (India)
1980 T. Tulasne (France)
1981 M. W. Anger (U.S.A.)
1982 P. Cash (Australia)
1983 S. Edberg (Sweden)
1984 M. Kratzmann (Australia)
1985 L. Lavalle (Mexico)
1986 E. Velez (Mexico)
1987 D. Nargiso (Italy)
1988 N. Pereira (Venezuela)

1989 N. Kulti (Sweden)
1990 L. Paes (India)
1991 T. Enquist (Sweden)
1992 D. Skoch (Czechoslovakia)
1993 R. Sabau (Romania)
1994 S. Humphries (U.S.A.)
1995 O. Mutis (France)
1996 V. Voltchkov (Belarus)
1997 W. Whitehouse (South Africa)
1998 R. Federer (Switzerland)
1999 J. Melzer (Austria)
2000 N. Mahut (France)
2001 R. Valent (Switzerland)
2002 T. Reid (Australia)

BOYS' DOUBLES

1982 P. Cash and J. Frawley
1983 M. Kratzmann and S. Youl
1984 R. Brown and R. Weiss
1985 A. Moreno and J. Yzaga
1986 T. Carbonell and P. Korda
1987 J. Stoltenberg and T. Woodbridge

1988 J. Stoltenberg and T. Woodbridge
1989 J. Palmer and J. Stark
1990 S. Lareau and S. Leblanc
1991 K. Alami and G. Rusedski
1992 S. Baldas and S. Draper
1993 S. Downs and J. Greenhalgh

1994 B. Ellwood and M. Philippoussis
1995 M. Lee and J.M. Trotman
1996 D. Bracciali and J. Robichaud
1997 L. Horna and N. Massu
1998 R. Federer and O. Rochus
1999 G. Coria and D. Nalbandian

2000 D. Coene and K. Vliegen
2001 F. Dancevic and G. Lapentti
2002 F. Mergea and H. Tecau

GIRLS' SINGLES

1947 Miss B. Domken (Belgium)
1948 Miss O. Miskova (Czechoslovakia)
1949 Miss C. Mercelis (Belgium)
1950 Miss L. Cornell (G.B.)
1951 Miss L. Cornell (G.B.)
1952 Miss ten Bosch (Netherlands)
1953 Miss D. Kilian (S.A.)
1954 Miss V.A. Pitt (G.B.)
1955 Miss S. M. Armstrong (G.B.)
1956 Miss A. S. Haydon (G.B.)
1957 Miss M. Arnold (U.S.A.)
1958 Miss S. M. Moore (U.S.A.)
1959 Miss J. Cross (S.A.)
1960 Miss K. Hantze (U.S.A.)

1961 Miss G. Baksheeva (U.S.S.R.)
1962 Miss G. Baksheeva (U.S.S.R.)
1963 Miss D. M. Salfati (France)
1964 Miss P. Bartkowicz (U.S.A.)
1965 Miss O. Morozova (U.S.S.R.)
1966 Miss B. Lindstrom (Finland)
1967 Miss J. Salome (Netherlands)
1968 Miss K. Pigeon (U.S.A.)
1969 Miss K. Sawamatsu (Japan)
1970 Miss S. Walsh (U.S.A.)
1971 Miss M. Kroschina (U.S.S.R.)
1972 Miss I. Kloss (S.A.)
1973 Miss A. Kiyomura (U.S.A.)
1974 Miss M. Jausovec (Yugoslavia)

1975 Miss N.Y. Chmyreva (U.S.S.R.)
1976 Miss N.Y. Chmyreva (U.S.S.R.)
1977 Miss I. Antonoplis (U.S.A.)
1978 Miss T. Austin (U.S.A.)
1979 Miss M. L. Piatek (U.S.A.)
1980 Miss D. Freeman (Australia)
1981 Miss Z. Garrison (U.S.A.)
1982 Miss C. Tanvier (France)
1983 Miss P. Paradis (France)
1984 Miss A. N. Croft (G.B.)
1985 Miss A. Holikova (Czechoslovakia)
1986 Miss N. Zvereva (U.S.S.R.)
1987 Miss N. Zvereva (U.S.S.R.)
1988 Miss B. Schultz (Netherlands)

1989 Miss A. Strnadova (Czechoslavakia)
1990 Miss A. Strnadova (Czechoslavakia)
1991 Miss B. Rittner (Germany)
1992 Miss C. Rubin (U.S.A.)
1993 Miss N. Feber (Belgium)
1994 Miss M. Hingis (Switzerland)
1995 Miss A. Olsza (Poland)
1996 Miss A. Mauresmo (France)
1997 Miss C. Black (Zimbabwe)
1998 Miss K. Srebotnik (Slovenia)
1999 Miss I. Tulyagnova (Uzbekhistan)
2000 Miss M. E. Salerni (Argentina)
2001 Miss A. Widjaja (Indonesia)
2002 Miss V. Douchevina (Russia)

GIRLS' DOUBLES

1982 Miss B. Herr and Miss P. Barg
1983 Miss P. Fendick and Miss P. Hy
1984 Miss C. Kuhlman and Miss S. Rehe
1985 Miss L. Field and Miss J. Thompson
1986 Miss M. Jaggard and Miss L. O'Neill
1987 Miss N. Medvedeva and Miss N. Zvereva

1988 Miss J. A. Faull and Miss R. McQuillan
1989 Miss J. Capriati and Miss M. McGrath
1990 Miss K. Habsudova and Miss A. Strnadova
1991 Miss C. Barclay and Miss L. Zaltz
1992 Miss M. Avotins and Miss L. McShea
1993 Miss L. Courtois and Miss N. Feber

1994 Miss E. De Villiers and Miss E. E. Jelfs
1995 Miss C. Black and Miss A. Olsza
1996 Miss O. Barabanschikova and Miss A. Mauresmo
1997 Miss C. Black and Miss I. Selyutina
1998 Miss E. Dyrberg and Miss J. Kostanic
1999 Miss D. Bedanova and Miss M.E. Salerni

2000 Miss I. Gaspar and Miss T. Perebiynis
2001 Miss G. Dulko and Miss A. Harkleroad
2002 Miss E. Clijsters and Miss B. Strycova